The Reith Lectures

The Reith Lectures were inaugurated in 1948 by the BBC as a 'stimulus to thought and contribution to knowledge' and has remained a flagship programme in Radio 4's broadcasting ever since. In an era of twenty-four-hour news and shortened attention spans, the series gives rare space and time for brilliant and entertaining people to develop their ideas and arguments.

The name marks the historic contribution made to public service broadcasting by Lord Reith, the founder of the BBC. John Reith maintained that broadcasting should be a public service which 'enriches the intellectual and cultural life of the nation'. It is in this spirit that the BBC each year invites a leading figure to deliver a series of lectures on radio, aiming to advance public understanding and debate about significant issues of contemporary interest.

The first BBC Reith lecturer was the philosopher, Bertrand Russell, and in the seventy years since there have been seventy-seven different speakers. Nineteen lecturers feature in this volume, spanning topics across art, science, nature, technology, history, religion, society, culture and politics, and in each case a highlight essay from their lecture series has been chosen.

Remarkable Minds

A Celebration of the Reith Lectures

BBC Radio 4

HEADLINE

First published in 2019 by
HEADLINE PUBLISHING GROUP

1

Cataloguing in Publication Data is available from the British Library

Hardback ISBN 978 1 4722 6228 8
Trade paperback ISBN 978 1 4722 6230 1

Designed and typeset by EM&EN
Printed and bound in Great Britain by Clays Ltd, Elcograf S.p.A.

HEADLINE PUBLISHING GROUP
An Hachette UK Company
Carmelite House
50 Victoria Embankment
London EC4Y 0DZ

www.headline.co.uk
www.hachette.co.uk

Contents

Foreword

Anita Anand

June 2019

Anita Anand is a broadcaster, journalist, author and the presenter of the Reith Lectures. Her predecessor, Sue Lawley, hosted for seventeen years before handing over to Anita in 2018 for Professor Margaret MacMillan's series 'The Mark of Cain'.

A former controller of Radio 4 once told me that running the station was much like carrying fine bone china across a highly polished floor. One wrong step and a priceless heirloom would come crashing to the ground. Moreover, your entire family would hate you for ever. It is a funny but rather appropriate observation. People associated with Radio 4 tend to care a lot. Be they presenters like me, producers, researchers, management or listeners, when it comes to this station we all share a powerful sense of ownership.

To extend the metaphor, the Reith Lectures represent

the family silver; they are elegant, beautifully crafted and extremely valuable. The lectures are polished for months at a time, and brought out to gleam once a year. They are shared with the very best guests. Those who tune in have curious minds, a fierce desire to learn, and the confidence to have their opinions challenged. It has been this way for more than seven decades.

I remember exactly where I was when Gwyneth Williams, my Radio 4 controller at the time, rang in 2018, to ask whether I would consider becoming the new presenter of 'the Reiths'. It meant stepping into the shoes of the redoubtable Sue Lawley and her offer knocked the wind right out of me. It just so happened I had been grocery shopping, and was making my way home at the time. I found myself putting my shopping on a bench and walking away from it when it became clear what was being asked. Somehow, it did not feel seemly to have such an important conversation in front of my comestibles.

I had been a devoted listener to the Reith Lectures for many years. Indeed, I had been a member of the audience for a live recording just a few years earlier. Like hundreds of others that day, I sat rapt in London's Royal Institution, listening to what would be one of Sir Stephen Hawking's last public addresses. I felt I was witnessing history from my chair in the fourteenth row. Now, to be offered a ringside seat as the presenter of the Reiths was an extraordinary privilege. I will be forever grateful for Gwyneth's call.

The Reith Lectures are, and have always been, important. They underpin the very ethos of the organisation I am proud to work for. They embody public service broadcasting in its purest form. Lord Reith, the BBC's first Director General, had wanted to create programmes which 'enriched the intellectual and cultural life of the nation'; the series created in his name has done that and so much more over seventy years.

In the beginning there was Bertrand Russell. Invited in 1948 to deliver the first ever lecture, the man who would win the Nobel Prize for Literature two years later chose as his subject: 'Authority and the Individual'. Later described as something of a 'lofty pacifist', Russell would that year become notorious for arguing that it would be morally worse to deploy military might against the USSR *after* they possessed the atomic bomb than *before*. His Reith Lectures seemed to be laying the grounds for a first strike against the Soviets. According to Russell's reckoning, while the USSR had no bomb, the West's victory would be swift and incur fewer casualties. It was right to use might, he reasoned.

Russell's lectures were not, shall we say, universally acclaimed. Moscow, quite understandably, saw his words as a direct attack on them and all they stood for. As far as the Kremlin was concerned, the philosopher had issued a clarion call to any who hated Communism. Lord Reith was similarly unimpressed, but for very different reasons. It was Russell's delivery rather than the content of his lecture which offended him. Writing about his inaugural speaker in his diary, Lord

Reith noted scathingly: 'Listened to the first Reith lecture by Bertrand Russell, forsooth. He went far too quickly and has a bad voice. However I wrote him a civil note.'

Though we do not have written evidence of a Reithian 'forsooth' for George Kennan's lecture in 1957, we do know that the former US ambassador's contribution mollified the Soviet Union after Russell had so successfully ruffled its fur. Contrary to the popular view at the time, Kennan argued that negotiation with Russia was imperative. Military action, he insisted, would not be able to contain the spread of communism. Kennan's Reith Lectures upset many of his peers, both in Washington and London, particularly when he suggested that the allies should withdraw their troops from Germany completely. As the West wrapped itself against the chill of the Cold War, with his lectures, Kennan had effectively thrown diplomatic dynamite into the brazier.

The Reith Lectures have always had the power to rattle the most rarefied circles. During my second year as the presenter, our Reith lecturer, the former Supreme Court Judge Lord Sumption (included in this volume), was answering questions from members of the audience. This public interaction is a vital part of the Reith broadcasts, and often yields unexpected results.

Just one year earlier, lawyers for Noel Conway, a retired lecturer paralysed from the neck down by progressive motor neurone disease, argued that the 1961 Suicide Act, criminalising anyone assisting a death, was incompatible with his human rights. Conway's appeal, an attempt to prevent end-of-life suffering, was dismissed. Raising that case, a member of our audience shared a powerful piece of emotional testimony: she was a widow who had been investigated by police for accompanying her terminally ill husband to DIGNITAS, a Swiss assisted–dying facility. She wanted to know if Lord Sumption thought the law was just. Reminding him of the pain it had caused her, she asked: could he still stand by it?

I felt a collective intake of breath when Sumption, in the grand setting of London's Middle Temple Hall, told her that though he stood by that legislation which had caused her so much anguish, he also believed people like her had 'no moral obligation to obey that law'. At first I thought I had heard him incorrectly. Was a former Supreme Court judge really encouraging people to break the law if they disagreed with it? Perhaps sensing the confusion his words had caused, Lord Sumption went on to make his point even more clearly: 'I think the law should continue to criminalise assisted suicide,' he said, adding: 'And I think that the law should be broken from time to time.' Unsurprisingly, the papers were very taken with that particular story.

The Reith Lectures are often controversial, but they have also proven themselves to be remarkably prescient too. In 1949 Sir Robert Birley, an English educationalist and anti-apartheid campaigner – 'Red Robert' to those offended by his views – gave a series of Reith Lectures musing on the prospect and benefits of a 'European Union'. The titles of his lectures: 'The

Problems of Patriotism'; 'The Meeting of Britain and Europe'; 'Problem of a Common Language'; and 'Britain's contribution to a European Society', would not seem out of place in a broadsheet editorial today, yet they were voiced a full forty-four years before the creation of the European Union.

In 1972, the British Economist and author of *Modern Capitalism*, Andrew Shonfield (included in this volume) picked up the thread from Birley. His lecture was altogether less esoteric because Britain was on the cusp of joining the European Community just two months later. The timing gave Shonfield's lectures a real sense of urgency and import.

The Reith Lectures not only reflect the time in which they were delivered, but often take a scalpel to the insecurities faced by the world at that given moment. Topics have ranged from concrete to abstract, and have included Britain's place in the world, nuclear tension, globalisation, terrorism as well as music, art and the limits of imagination.

In 1952, the author, philosopher and historian Arnold Toynbee asked listeners to consider the impact of Westernisation in Islamic countries. Ten years later George Carstairs, the psychiatrist and professor of Psychological Medicine, was identifying reasons why teenagers were drawn to violence and sex for a mystified and slightly appalled Radio 4 listenership. Carstairs managed to cause widespread outrage when he said that young people in the 1960s saw sexual experience as 'a sensible preliminary to marriage' and pointed out that 'many societies get on quite well without premarital chastity'.

Foreword

Looking at the roster of previous Reith speakers and their subject matter, I sometimes wonder what they would think of us now, and how listeners might judge our engagement with and response to lectures past. I imagine those who tuned into the English ecologist Frank Fraser Darling in 1969, warning about the dangers of global warming, might shake their heads in disappointment if they were to learn that fifty years later we have, in the words of the United Nations, brought the world to a place where it is facing a 'climate catastrophe'.

Though the subject matter of the Reith Lectures has certainly been diverse, that cannot always have been said of the lecturers. Initially they were exclusively male until Margery Perham, the colonial historian, delivered her lectures in 1961. They were also all white. Robert Gardiner, the Ghanaian professor and economist, who served with the United Nations, broke the mould in 1965, when he delivered his series of lectures considering the state of race relations internationally. Since then, the effort to find diverse voices from a spread of disciplines, with a wealth of different experiences has been tangible and a real credit to successive Radio 4 controllers.

I had the great pleasure of hosting the Canadian historian Margaret MacMillan as my first Reith Lecturer, for her series on the nature of war and its impact on human society. An Oxford professor and respected author, who also happens to be the great-granddaughter of former British Prime Minister David Lloyd George, on paper Margaret was an intimidating prospect. Yet in person, she could not have been more charming. It was not long before she was sharing a rather unusual story which might have been the seed for her fascination with war. It turned out that as a child, she and her siblings had played with a grenade her grandfather had brought back from his time serving as a doctor on the Western Front during the First World War. In her distinctive mid-Atlantic, understated tone she mused: 'You know, I never really think anyone checked if the pin was still in. I suppose someone really should have done that, shouldn't they?'

Margaret's lectures took us all over the world. We travelled to Belfast, where former paramilitaries from both sides sat just inches from each other and listened to what she had to say, then to Beirut, which still wears the bullet marks of its bitter civil war in the walls of its buildings. The locations added greatly to the sense of occasion for both, and it is another hallmark of the Reith Lectures that apart from being broadcast all over the world, they attempt to visit different countries and 'speak truth to power' in a variety of different places.

It was rather delicious, for example, to see Lord Sumption, with a distinct twinkle in his eye, tell the Americans in Washington all the failings of their written constitution. I asked him later whether it had been a bit 'Old World Smug' to travel all the way to the States and spend his time cataloguing all the shortcomings of their system of government. 'Well we have to learn from everyone's mistakes,' he said, somewhat impishly.

I have witnessed one common thing among my wonderful Reith lecturers: they really care about the words they will share with the world. Though they may have achieved greatness in their fields, they still craft and hone their thoughts right until the moment they take to that lectern and the microphones are switched on. At that moment, a certain magic takes place. They seem to grow a few inches before my eyes. Any hint of 'pre-match nerves' dissolves in an instant, replaced by a tone which I know will command the attention of millions. The Reith lecturers understand only too well the important part they play in this extraordinary seventy-year-old relay race. I for one cannot wait to see who takes up the baton next year, and which direction he or she will lead us.

Introduction

‎—⁀—

Gwyneth Williams

May 2019

Gwyneth Williams was controller of BBC Radio 4 from
2010–2019. She spent forty-three years with the corpo-
ration, having joined the BBC World Service as a trainee
in 1976.

'The Reiths', as we call them, have become personal. It seems
as if I have measured out my time at the BBC in Reith Lectures
– and Reith lecturers – having first edited then commissioned
the series over many years. I have stories to tell about my
lecturers. Some have become friends and all have my respect
and affection.

Editing, commissioning and travelling together creates a
special bond, not just with the lecturer but often with their
friends and family. Wole Soyinka, for instance, always carried
a small pot of chilli with which to spice the bland English food
often served in formal Reith dinners. He would reach into his

shirt pocket and produce it, offering it round the table before we ate. Sometimes Reith lecturers have introduced future Reith lecturers. Daniel Barenboim invited Anthony Appiah to his Reith dinner in the US, telling me about Anthony's book *Cosmopolitanism*. I read it and kept in touch with Anthony over many years, meeting during New York visits and then, exactly ten years later in 2016, he presented his series on identity politics, 'Mistaken Identities'.

It took me some time to persuade Daniel Barenboim to deliver his lectures on music and society. 'What?' he said when I asked him during a special trip to Vienna that I undertook in order to persuade him, 'You want me to talk? People will say why doesn't he shut up and play the piano . . .' His lectures were among my favourite and I will always be grateful to him for changing forever the way I listen to music. It was my privilege as editor to travel and work with such an inspiring and remarkable man. He took me to a memorable rehearsal in Ramallah of his Young Palestine Chamber Orchestra while recording one of the lectures and I managed to iron the shirt of the pianist before he played. I felt as proud of that young man as of my own son (of similar age and also a pianist) filled with music, youth and hope.

Onora O'Neill's 2002 series on the crisis of trust in public institutions was possibly the most influential of all the lecture series with which I have been associated and they are still frequently quoted. I remember going to Newnham College in Cambridge and sitting in her study with a ruler as we went through her script line by line. She is formidable and was the first person to mention to me the issue of Ireland at the very start of the current Brexit discussions, way ahead of anyone else.

Wole's lecture series too was ahead of events. I worked with him to turn a long script into four distinct lectures over a tense weekend in California while the Santa Ana winds blew great fires closer and closer to my hotel. I sat alone working on the script while ash fell into the pool beneath my window and families and dogs arrived at the hotel for refuge. His Atlanta lecture was entitled 'I am Right, You are Dead' and his overall title was 'The Climate of Fear'. This title we had to argue for with the then Controller of Radio 4, I recall, but consider how perspicacious it was in 2004, less than three years after 9/11 and before global terrorism had become an accepted part of modern life.

Aung San Suu Kyi's lectures had to be smuggled out of Burma as she delivered them before she was released from house arrest, at a time when she was universally admired and her voice seldom heard. Her live responses to questions from the audience, gathered in the Radio Theatre at Broadcasting House, were made on a distant phone line from Burma when, in a dramatic moment, the electricity failed and she was plunged into darkness far away and alone.

Each lecture series has its memorable moments. Eliza Manningham-Buller (included in this volume), talking about security ten years after 9/11, as the former head of MI5, replied as follows to a question from the Minister-Counsellor at the Russian embassy. Her tone was brisk: 'Can I suggest when you next have guests to the Lubyanka that you install a ladies cloakroom . . .' She concluded drily – this was no joke – as laughter erupted, 'I much enjoyed my visit there, but there was no ladies'.'

Grayson Perry satirised the lectures winningly, if savagely, with a series of cartoons accompanying his Reiths, one of which featured a Lowry-style sketch with penis-shaped factory towers emitting blasts of hot air spelling out 'Reith Lectures' in clouds. I commissioned Grayson to give his series more or less on the spot over dinner at the British Museum after an inspiring conversation with him about the nature of creativity.

Sue Lawley chaired the series from 2000 to 2017. She brought a sharp journalistic edge to the subject matter, often puncturing tendencies sometimes displayed by academics to take themselves too seriously. In her masterful way as a star presenter she represented the audience, the discerning and intelligent Radio 4 listeners who want to learn from the lectures and also to enjoy themselves and be part of an event based around current thinking. Unfailingly elegant, Sue would put me to shame as we travelled: she cool and stylish and me rather more rumpled. 'Keep up; keep up,' she called as she took me for my first ever jog in Central Park many years ago. That was always a losing battle but we have remained friends ever since.

I was given the lectures to edit when I was Head of Radio

Introduction

Current Affairs by the then Controller of Radio 4, James Boyle. I broadcast them on the World Service when I was there as Director of the English World Service and in recent years I have commissioned and broadcast them as Controller of Radio 4. The Reiths are something special in Radio 4's calendar. They are the Controller's biggest editorial statement of the year, broadcast in prime time at 9 a.m., and stretching over four or five weeks, reaching millions of listeners both on air and as downloads or podcasts. If they are well-judged they have an impact way beyond the broadcasts, influencing the public debate with new ideas. They are unique in that they argue a single theme over four or five lectures and thus they keep the focus on trends below the surface of news and events.

I had an exchange around the time of writing this introduction with Anthony Giddens (then Director of the LSE and the thinker behind the 'Third Way' from the Tony Blair years) who gave the first Reith lecturers that I was involved with in 1999 on the theme of globalisation. We were some way ahead of events as, indeed, the Reiths should be. However, the title of that series could not be more appropriate today. It was 'Runaway World'.

As I said at the start of this introduction, the Reiths have become personal. I have chosen to end my tenure as Controller Radio 4 with Jonathan Sumption's impressive 2019 series on law and the decline of politics, included in this collection. The lectures have come to stand for what I most believe in in my job. Ideas have the power to change the world. Radio 4 takes ideas seriously and it is our public service duty to bring them to our audience and explore them in depth. Our audience in the UK and around the world deserves the highest quality programmes from the BBC as they seek to understand the world and make decisions about how they want to live and how to structure our societies. The Reith Lectures stand at the heart of public service broadcasting and they represent the core of my endeavour while Controller as being above all to keep Radio 4 intelligent.

2019

Jonathan Sumption

Law and the Decline of Politics

Extract from 'Law's Expanding Empire'

Lord Jonathan Sumption (born 1948), is a British judge, author and historian. His Reith Lecture series explored the place of law in public life, outlining the decline of politics and the rise of law to fill the void. In this first lecture, delivered from Middle Temple Hall in London, Lord Sumption discusses how growth of the law, driven by demand for greater security and less risk, means we have less liberty.

In the beginning, there was chaos and brute force, a world without law. In the mythology of ancient Athens, Agamemnon sacrificed his daughter so that the gods would allow his fleet to sail against Troy. His wife murdered him to avenge the deed, and she in turn was murdered by her son. Athena, the goddess of wisdom, put an end to the cycle of violence by creating a court to impose a solution, in what today we would call the public interest: a solution based on reason, on the experience of human frailty, and on fear of the alternative. In the final part of Aeschylus's great trilogy the *Oresteia*, the goddess justifies her intervention in the world of mortals in these words: 'Let no man live uncurbed by law, nor curbed by tyranny.' That was written in the fifth century BC. But the message is timeless and universal. Law is not just an instrument of corrective or distributive justice. It is an expression of collective values and an alternative to violence and capricious despotism.

It is a vice of some lawyers that they talk about law as if it was a self-contained subject, something to be examined like a laboratory specimen in a test tube. But law does not occupy a world of its own. It is part of a larger system of public decision-making. The rest is politics: the politics of ministers and legislators; of political parties; of media and pressure groups; and of the wider electorate.

What ought to be the role of law in a representative democracy like ours? Is there too much law? Is there, perhaps, too little? Do judges have too much power? What do we mean by the rule of law, the phrase which so readily trips off the tongues of lawyers? Is it, as cynics have suggested, really no more than a euphemism for the rule of lawyers?

The expanding empire of law is one of the most significant phenomena of our time. This magnificent hall has been used by lawyers since it was built four and a half centuries ago. But for most of that time, they had very little to do. Until the nineteenth century, most human social interactions were governed by custom and convention. The law dealt with a very narrow range of human problems. It regulated title to property. It enforced contracts. It protected people's lives, their persons, their liberty and their property against arbitrary injury. But that was about all. Today, law penetrates every corner of human life. The standard modern edition of the English statutes fills fifty stout volumes, with more than thirty volumes of supplements. In addition, there are currently about 21,000 regulations made by ministers under statutory powers, and nearly 12,000 regulations made by the European Union, which will continue to apply until repealed or replaced by domestic legislation. In a single year, ending in May 2010, more than 700 new criminal offences were created, three quarters of them by government regulation.

That was admittedly a bumper year, but the rate of increase continues to be high.

On top of that, there is the relentless output of judgments of the courts, many of them on subjects which were hardly touched by law a century ago. The powers of the family courts now extend to every aspect of the well-being of children, which once belonged to the enclosed domain of the home. Complex codes of law, enforced by specialised tribunals, regulate the world of employment. An elaborate system of administrative law, largely developed by judges since the 1960s, governs most aspects of the relations between government and the citizen. The special areas which were once thought to be outside the purview of the courts, such as foreign policy, the conduct of overseas military operations and the other prerogative powers of the state, have one by one yielded to the power of judges. Above all, since 2000 a code of legally enforceable human rights has opened up vast new areas to judicial regulation. The impact of these changes can be measured by the growth of the legal profession. In 1911 there was one solicitor in England for every 3,000 inhabitants. Just over a century later, there is about one for every 400, a sevenfold increase.

The rule of law is one of those clichés of modern life which tends to be invoked, even by lawyers, without much reflection on what it actually means. The essence of it can be summed up in three points. First, public authorities have no power to coerce us, other than what the law gives them. Second, people must have a minimum of basic legal rights. One can argue about what those rights should be. But they must at least include protection from physical violence and from arbitrary interference with life, liberty and property. Without these, social existence is no more than a crude contest in the deployment of force. Third, there must be access to independent judges to vindicate these rights, administer the criminal law and enforce the limits of state power. At least as important as these, however, is a clear understanding of what the rule of law does not mean. It does not mean that every human problem and every moral dilemma calls for a legal solution. So, why has this vast expansion of the domain of law happened?

The fundamental reason is the arrival of a broadly based democracy between the 1860s and the 1920s. Mass involvement in public affairs has inevitably led to rising demands of the state: as the provider of amenities, as a guarantor of minimum standards of security, and as a regulator of economic activity. Optimism about what collective action can achieve is natural to social animals. Law is the prime instrument of collective action, and rising expectations of the state lead naturally to calls for legal solutions.

In some areas, a legal solution is dictated by the nature of the problem. Take, for example, the unwelcome side-effects of technological and economic change, what economists call 'externalities': industrial sickness and injury, pollution, monopoly, climate change, to name only some of the more obvious ones. Economic growth is the spontaneous creation of numberless individuals. But spontaneous action cannot address the unwanted collective costs that go with it. Only the state can do that. So we have laws against cartels, pollution, and so on. However, there are other areas where the intervention of law is not forced on us. It is a collective choice, which reflects pervasive changes in our outlook. I want to draw attention to two of these changes which have, I think, contributed a great deal to the expansion of law's empire. One is a growing moral and social absolutism which looks to law to produce social and moral conformity. The other is the constant quest for greater security and reduced risk.

Let us look first at law as a means of imposing conformity. This was once regarded as one of its prime functions. The law regulated religious worship until the eighteenth century. It discriminated between different religious denominations until the nineteenth. It regulated private and consensual sexual relations until quite recently. Homosexual acts were criminal until 1967. Today the law has almost entirely withdrawn from these areas. Indeed, it has moved to the opposite extreme and banned the discrimination that was once compulsory.

Yet in other respects, we have moved back to the old idea that law exists to impose conformity. We live in a censorious age, more so perhaps than at any time since the evangelical movement transformed the moral sensibilities of the Victorians. Liberal voices in Victorian Britain, like John Stuart Mill, were already protesting against the implications for personal liberty. Law, he argued, exists to protect us from harm, not to recruit us to moral conformity. Yet today a hectoring press can discharge an avalanche of public scorn and abuse on anyone who steps out of line. Social media encourage a resort to easy answers, and generate a powerful herd instinct which suppresses not just dissent but even doubt and nuance. Public and even private solecisms can destroy a person's livelihood. Advertisers pressurise editors not to publish controversial pieces, and editors can be sacked for persisting. Student organisations can prevent unorthodox speakers from being heard. These things have made the pressure to conform more intense than it ever was in Mill's day. This is the same mentality which looks to law to regulate areas of life which once belonged exclusively to the domain of personal judgment. We are a lot less ready than we were to respect the autonomy of an individual's choices. We tend to regard social and moral values as belonging to the community as a whole, as matters for collective and not personal decision.

Two years ago, the courts and the press were much exercised by the case of Charlie Gard, a baby who had been born with a rare and fatal genetic disease. The medical advice was that there was no appreciable chance of improvement. The hospital where he was being treated applied to the High Court for permission to withdraw treatment and allow him to die. The parents rejected the medical advice. They wanted to take him out of the hands of the NHS and move him to the United States so that he could receive an untested experimental treatment there. The American specialist thought that the chances of improvement were small, but better than zero. The parents wanted to take the chance. Unusually, they had raised the money by crowdfunding, and were able to pay the cost without resorting to public funds. The case raised a difficult combination of moral judgment and pragmatic welfare. The courts authorised the hospital to withdraw therapeutic treatment and the child died.

Now there are two striking features of this story. The first is that although the decision whether to continue treatment was a matter of clinical judgment, the clinicians involved were unwilling to make that judgment on their own, as I suspect they would have done a generation before. They wanted the endorsement of a judge. This was not because judges were thought to have any special clinical or moral qualifications that the doctors lacked. It was because judges have a power of absolution. By passing the matter to the courts the doctors sheltered themselves from legal liability. That is an understandable instinct. Doctors do not want to run the risk of being sued or prosecuted, however confident they are of their judgment. But the risk of being sued or prosecuted only exists because we have come to regard these terrible human dilemmas as the proper domain of law.

The second feature of the case is perhaps even more striking. The courts ruled that not only should the hospital be entitled to withdraw therapeutic treatment, but the parents should not be permitted to take the chance of a cure elsewhere. It was not suggested that moving him to the United

States and treating him there would actually worsen his awful situation, although it would obviously have prolonged it. The parents' judgment seems to have been within the broad range of judgments which responsible and caring parents could make. Yet in law it was ultimately a matter for an organ of the state, namely the Family Division of the High Court. The parents' decision was, so to speak, nationalised. I should make it clear that I am not criticising this decision. I only point out that the decision would probably have been different a generation before, if indeed the question had reached the courts at all.

I cite this agonising case because although its facts are unusual, it is illustrative of a more general tendency of law. Rules of law and the discretionary powers which the law confers on judges limit the scope for autonomous decision-making by individuals. They cut down the area within which citizens take personal responsibility for their own destinies and those of their families. Of course, the law has always done this in some areas. The classic liberal position (again, it was John Stuart Mill who expressed it best) is that we have to distinguish between those acts which affect other people, and are therefore proper matters for legal regulation; and those which only affect the actor, which belong in his personal space. So, we criminalise murder, rape, theft and fraud. We say that the morality of these acts is not something that should be left to the conscience of every individual. Not only are they harmful to others, but there is an almost complete consensus that they are morally wrong. What is new is the growing tendency for law to regulate human choices even in cases where they do no harm to others, and there is no consensus about their morality.

A good example is provided by some recent animal welfare legislation. Take fur farming. England and Scotland, in common with some other European countries, have, over the last few years, banned fur farming. The reason is not that the farming and humane slaughter of furry animals for human use are themselves objectionable. Most people accept that rearing and killing animals for food, for example, is morally acceptable. But we don't eat beavers or minks. The sole reason for farming them is their fur. The idea behind the statutory ban is that the desire to wear a beaver hat or a mink coat is not a morally sufficient reason for killing animals, whereas a desire to eat them would be. Yet many people would disagree with that judgment. Some of them are happy to wear fur even if others disagree. But Parliament has decreed that fur farming is not a matter on which they should be allowed to make their own moral judgments. Similar points could be made about the elaborate legislation which now regulates the docking of dog's tails. It allows the practice where it has a utilitarian value (for working dogs for example) but not where its only value is aesthetic (for household pets or dog shows).

Now, I don't want to get into an argument about the rights or wrongs of laws like these. I am genuinely neutral about that. The point that I am making is a different one. These laws are addressed to moral issues on which people hold a variety of different views. But the law regulates their moral choices on the principle that there ought to be only one collective moral judgment, not a multiplicity of individual ones. This tells us something about the changing attitude of our society to law. It marks the expansion of the public space at the expense of the private space that was once thought sacrosanct. Even when there are no compelling welfare considerations involved, we resort to law to impose uniform solutions in areas where we once tolerated a diversity of judgment and behaviour. We are afraid to let people be guided by their own moral judgments, in case they arrive at answers that we do not agree with.

Let us turn now to the other major factor behind the growing public appetite for legal rules, namely the quest for greater security and reduced risk. This is particularly important in the areas of public order, health and safety, employment, and consumer protection, which present the main risks to our well-being and account for a high proportion of modern lawmaking.

People sometimes speak as if the elimination of risk to life, health and well-being was an absolute value. But we do not really act on that principle, either in our own lives or in our collective arrangements. Think about road accidents. They are by far the largest cause of accidental physical injury in this country. We could almost completely eliminate them by reviving the Locomotive Act of 1865, which limited the speed of motorised vehicles to four miles an hour in the country and two in towns. Today we allow faster speeds, although we know for certain that it will mean many more people being killed or injured. We do this because total safety would be too inconvenient. Difficult as it is to say so, hundreds of deaths on the roads and thousands of crippling injuries are thought to be a price worth paying for the ability to get around quicker and more comfortably. So eliminating risk is not an absolute value. It is a question of degree.

Some years ago, the courts had to deal with the case of a young man who had broken his neck by diving into a shallow lake at a well-known beauty spot. He was paralysed for life. He sued the local authority for negligence. The local authority had put up warning notices. But his case was that since they knew that people were apt to ignore warning notices, they should have taken steps to close off the lake area altogether. The Court of Appeal agreed with him. But when the case reached the House of Lords, the judges pointed out that there was a price to be paid for protecting this young man from his own folly. The price was the loss of liberty which would be suffered by the great majority of people who enjoyed visiting the lake and were sensible enough to do it safely. So the claim ultimately failed.

The Law Lords had put their fingers on a wider dilemma. Every time that a public authority is blamed for failing to prevent some tragedy like this, it will tend to respond by restricting the liberty of the public at large in order to deprive them of the opportunity to harm themselves. It is the only sure way to deflect criticism. Every time that we criticise social workers for failing to stop some terrible instance of child abuse, we are in effect inviting them to intervene more readily in the lives of innocent parents in case their children too may be at risk. The law can enhance personal security. But its protection comes at a price, and it can be a heavy one. Thus we arrive at one of the supreme ironies of modern life: we have expanded the range of individual rights, while at the same time drastically curtailing the scope for individual choice.

Dilemmas of this sort have existed for centuries. What has changed in recent years is the degree of risk that people are prepared to tolerate in their lives. Unlike our forebears, we are no longer willing to accept the wheel of fortune as an ordinary incident of human existence. We regard physical, financial and emotional security not just as a normal state of affairs but as an entitlement. Some people will welcome this change. Others will deplore it. Most of us probably take different views about it at different moments of our lives. But none of us should be surprised. It is a rational response to important changes in our world. Improvements in the technical competence of humanity have given us more influence over our own and other people's well-being. But they have not been matched by corresponding improvements in our moral sensibilities or our solicitude for our neighbours. Misfortunes which seemed unavoidable to our ancestors, seem eminently avoidable to us. Once they are seen to be avoidable consequences of human agency, they tend to become a proper subject for the attribution of legal responsibility. So, after every disaster, we are apt to think that the law must either have been broken or be insufficiently robust. We look for a legal remedy: a lawsuit, a criminal prosecution, or more legislation. 'There ought to be a law against it,' is the universal cry. Usually there is, or soon will be.

Of course, the law does not in fact provide a solution for every misfortune. It expects people, within limits, to look after their own interests. It assumes that some risks may have to be accepted because the social and economic cost of eliminating them is just too high. However, public expectations are a powerful motor of legal development. Judges do not decide cases in accordance with the state of public opinion. But it is their duty to take account of the values of the society which they serve. Risk-aversion has become one of the most powerful of those values.

These gradual changes in our collective attitudes have important implications for the way that we govern ourselves. We cannot have more law without more state power to apply it. The great seventeenth-century political philosopher Thomas Hobbes believed that political communities surrendered their liberty to an absolute monarch in return for security. Hobbes has few followers today. But modern societies have gone a long way towards justifying his theories. We have made a Leviathan of the state, expanding and harnessing its power in order to reduce the risks that threaten our well-being. The seventeenth century may have abolished absolute monarchy. But the twentieth century created absolute democracy in its place.

How to limit and control the power of the state is an evergreen question. The modern state's monopoly of organised force and its growing technical capacity have made it a more urgent question for our age than it was for our ancestors. But the nature of the debate is inevitably different in a democracy. Our ancestors looked upon the state as an autonomous power, embodied in a powerful monarch and his ministers. It was natural for them to talk about the relations between the state and its citizens in 'us and them' terms. But in a democracy, the state is neither with us nor against us. It *is* us. This is why most of us are so ambivalent about it. We resent its power. We object to its intrusiveness. We criticise the arrogance of some of its agents and spokesmen. But our collective expectations depend for their fulfilment on its persistent intervention in almost every area of our lives. We don't like it, but we want it. The danger is that the demands of democratic majorities for state action may take forms which are profoundly objectionable, even oppressive, to individuals or whole sectors of our society.

Hilary Mantel

$\smile$

Resurrection: The Art and Craft

Extract from 'Adaptation'

Dame Hilary Mantel (born 1952), is a bestselling novelist and twice winner of the Booker Prize (for *Wolf Hall* and *Bring Up the Bodies*). Her Reith Lecture series focuses on history's hold on the imagination and the role it plays in our culture. In this final lecture, Mantel discusses how fiction changes when adapted for stage or screen, and how each medium draws a different potential from the original.

In the stage play of my novel *Wolf Hall*, Thomas Cromwell wants the young nobleman Harry Percy to take an oath to declare that he is not now, and never has been, secretly married to Anne Boleyn. But Harry Percy thinks they are married. He protests, 'You can't change the past.'

'Oh,' says Cromwell, 'the past changes all the time, Harry. And I'm going to show you how easily it can be altered.'

He then grabs the young man and bangs his head on the table, as if to knock out his old memories and make space for new. We all used to look forward to this scene, except the actor who played Harry Percy.

Until this point, Cromwell had been an entirely reasonable man. In the original novel, that scene is more complex. Cromwell persuades the Earl that he must do as he's told, because Cromwell represents the force of the future, and Harry Percy is a member of an economically illiterate warrior class whose day is over. Swept away on a flood of words, concussed by metaphorical rocks, the young man gives way.

Why the difference? The theatre craves action – but it's not just that. The novel craves it too. But the hardest thing to put on the page is something that happens suddenly. The theatre is superb at surprise. It offers us thought condensed into action, just as the cinema does: it also takes an image and springs it open, so something powerful and unexpected jumps out. It puts the dead back into circulation, within touching distance.

When half-forgotten names are spoken – the names of real people, who happen to be dead – they shiver in the air of the auditorium, resonating in time and space. It makes me ask, is it enough to commemorate the dead by carving their names in stone? Or should we go into an arena and shout them out loud?

Fiction, if well written, doesn't betray history, but opens up its essential nature to inspection. When fiction is turned into theatre, or into a film or TV, the same applies: there is no necessary treason. Each way of telling, each medium for telling, draws a different potential from the original. Adaptation, done well, is not a secondary process, a set of grudging compromises – but an act of creation in itself.

Indeed, the work of adaptation is happening every day; without it, we couldn't understand the past at all. An event occurs once: everything else is reiteration, a performance. When action is captured on film, it seems we have certainty about what happened. We can freeze the moment. Repeat it. But in fact, reality has already been framed. What's out of shot is lost to us. In the very act of observing and recording, a gap has opened between the event and its transcription. Every night as you watch the news, you can see story forming up. The repetitious gabble of the reporter on the spot is soon smoothed to a studio version. The unmediated account is edited into coherence. Cause and effect are demonstrated by the way we order our account. It gathers a subjective human dimension as it is analysed, discussed. We shovel meaning into it. The raw event is now processed. It is adapted into history.

Most of us spend our lives in adaptation, aware we have a secret self, and aware that it won't do. We send out a persona to represent us, to deal for us in public; there are two of us, one home and one away, one original and one adapted.

Now technology has multiplied ways to play with our identities. In online games, we can choose an avatar. We can proliferate, untied from physical limitation. Reality TV sets up scenes in which people mimic their real lives – but trimmed to a tidier pattern, and with a neater script. Watching them fumble to imitate themselves, we say, 'Ah, but they're not real actors.' Television and the theatre pick up a fact-based story before it's cold, and dramatise it.

The living being and her impersonator can share a space. In Shakespeare's day, they didn't put the current monarch on stage, but our present queen can view herself adapted into different bodies, on stage, on TV, in the cinema. Meanwhile her humble subjects must make do with faking themselves, photographing their own faces, then adapting the result till they have a self they like better. It's surprising novelists stay in the business, with so many keen amateurs in the lying game.

We writers console ourselves. We say, the media consume

stories so fast that demand is always greater than supply. Everything starts with us, we say, sitting in a room: solitary, day-dreaming, scratching away like a monk. We could adapt, we say, if the Middle Ages came back. A paper and pen will do to conjure a world. Our imagination, we say, needs no power supply. But really, we wish we had a camera and a crew. In ten seconds, the screen can show nuances of character or plot developments that in a novel, or on stage, would be impossible to depict. The cinema has a wonderful easy power to tell us where to look: this is your hero, the man the camera is following.

There is a difficulty for a novelist who writes about what we used to call 'great men': we want to keep the greatness, while making them human. You don't want to cut them down to size in a spiteful modern way – even if you don't admire them, you have to recognise that an individual plus a reputation is more than just a private person – he or she is owned by everyone. So on stage, and on the page, there is a nervous moment, before you bring in the big character – as it might be, Henry VIII, or Marilyn Monroe. The expectation of the audience is vast; can the actor live up to it?

On film, there need be no make-or-break moment. The problematic body can swim out of the background, as if from a psychic veil, a mist: or the viewer can take it in bit by bit – a spur, or a stiletto heel. We don't need a lookalike. The cinema creates a mythic identity. We watch a film all together, in the dark. We engage in collective dreaming. And we eat – we eat with our fingers, cheap, gratifying, baby food – as if suspending adult life and adult judgement, sinking entirely into the story we are told. The image has taken reason prisoner. Then we come out into the street and are angry with ourselves, for believing what we see. The cinema is excellent at verisimilitude but less good with the truth. Time's the enemy. There's a limit to how many complex events you can digest into the average length of a feature film.

It is a rare gift, to be able to find images to carry facts. We have explanatory devices – voice-overs, captions; they can add creative value, or they can be desperate measures which regress to the text. I think that what the adaptor must do is set aside the source – whether it's a history book or a novel – put down the text, and dream it. If you dream it, you might get it right, the spirit if not the letter; but if you are literal, you will set yourself up for failure. Mostly, as I take it, film-makers don't set out to lie. Draft One may tell the truth: but a casual rewrite, in a series of rewrites by different hands, can shake out the truth and shake in a lie. As an audience, we recognise that film has the tools to do a really bad job. So a whole industry has grown up, of resistance: an industry of carping and picking holes.

We need the pedants and the complainers, to drive us back to the sources, and to open debate about what people call 'real history', and how it is sold to us. But it's a mistake to focus on trivialities. The people who demand total accuracy usually do it from a position of ignorance. To satisfy them would mean too much destruction. It would be vandalism to dig up a twenty-first century garden, so you only show sixteenth-century plants. You can make a literal reproduction of an eighteenth-century chair but it doesn't bring an eighteenth-century person to sit on it.

Not that accuracy is to be discouraged. A faithful representation is one that is stabilised by physical reality. In portraits of great women of the sixteenth century, they have a characteristic way of standing: head up, back straight, hands folded at the waist. Put a modern woman into a replica of that costume, properly weighted, and she can't stand any other way. Reality has a coercive force. The body adapts, and the body underneath matters as much as the clothes on top. It's the same with dialogue. Pastiche is not creative. We don't need our characters to mouth the words of another century, but to possess the common knowledge of their era – so they don't say what they could never think.

Compared to viewers thirty years ago, we are swift and sophisticated consumers of narrative. We have seen so many stories on the screen, and eaten them so fast with our gaze. Television can make our familiar world hyper-real, lying to us that no camera is present. But we wished to be undeceived – so we evolved the mock-documentary, which makes fun of its own workings. The actors flick a furtive glance at the camera, mimicking the embarrassment of a real person, caught in the nefarious act of going about their day. It may be because we are used to this ironical mode – realism smirking at itself – that the dramatic reconstructions inserted into history programmes now look so earnest and clumsy. We can see its low budget impersonation, and we refuse to suspend belief.

In the theatre we seldom refuse, as long as the events we're shown have emotional truth. Schiller's play Maria Stuart, first produced in 1800, sets up a meeting between Mary Queen of Scots and Elizabeth I. In real life, these rival queens never met. But we recognise the dramatic need to put them in the same place: after all, they must have met in the space within their heads. They probably dreamed of each other, and the playwright joins us to the dream. The theatre allows us to be complicit in deception, without feeling guilt – because it doesn't disguise its artificiality. As with the cinema, we wait till the lights go down, then abdicate from our stubborn literal selves.

History is always trying to show itself to us. In the western tradition, drama was a mature art when the novel was still young. We have built theatres for centuries – special buildings for the specific purpose of repeating human experience with small variations. In these buildings, day by day, everything is the same but not the same.

To adapt a history for the stage you must make time and space obey your laws. If you are working from a novel, that fiction becomes the canonical text, standing in for history. The novelist has some advantages. His stage sets are built out of black marks on white paper. On the page, a cast of a hundred is as cheap as a cast of two. For the stage, the adaptor must reduce the personnel, for practical as well as artistic reasons. Cut down the number of characters and you must adapt the story, reorganise events so that one person stands in for another.

It takes skill to manage that shift so you are still telling the truth – though not the literal truth. All we have is what Shakespeare calls, 'the two hours' traffic of our stage.' However gripping the action, it's a sad truth that an audience gets restless at ten o'clock. They might crave to see the wedding or the execution, then the curtain call, but they don't want to miss their train, or go home on the night bus with the drunks.

Each art form works when it plays to its strengths, or at least understands its weaknesses. The screenwriter knows his director can populate a city, or whistle up a mob using computer-generated imagery. The playwright's mob is too meagre to be scary. His battle scene suffers because he only has four combatants and some clattery shields. It's tough if your story ends in a battle. But then, look at the climax of Richard III. No one forgets Richard yelling out his big offer: 'My kingdom for a horse.' But no one is going to bring him a horse, because the real and chilling end to his story has already happened in the tent on the eve of battle, when the souls of the dead gather to tell him that the game's up. 'The lights burn blue; it is now dead midnight.' Their intimate whisper is more final than the force of arms.

There is a way around the practical constraints – it is to use words as arrows that go straight to the heart of an audience. A stage play is a brilliant vehicle for the past, because it is a hazardous, unstable form, enacting history as it was made – breath by breath. The script sets parameters – this time, this place, this bod – but the actor is not a repetition machine. Every show is different. History becomes interactive. Without speaking – by clapping, by sighing, by laughter, or by silence (and there are different kinds of silence) – the audience directs the show, subtly adjusting the rhythm and nuance of what they see. The barrier that protects the actor is invisible, held in place only by the imagination of the onlookers. Reality can't be censored out. Sirens from the street cut through the mutter of Roman conspiracy, as if someone had anticipated Caesar's assassination and sent for an ambulance. In the Schiller drama I mentioned, Maria Stuart, there is an invented character who, towards the end of the play, stabs himself. In 2008 in Vienna, the play's audience were aghast at the rush of blood – it seemed so impressively real. It was. By some backstage muddle – by error, not malice – the stage knife had been replaced by a real knife. Next day, the actor was back on stage, patched up. Living and dead in the theatre, we are not safe from each other.

In King Lear, art brings a man to the edge of a cliff. Outcast, the blinded Duke of Gloucester comes, as he believes, to Dover, stumbling towards death. He thinks he has arrived the edge of England. He launches himself into the empty air. We, the audience, can see there is no cliff. The blind man is standing on solid ground. It's a trick adapted from low comedy, from farce – an old fool reacting to an imaginary peril. But then the truth comes home to us, in a pulse-beat: and not just the truth about the blind duke. The cliff is invisible, but real. That's where we all live, one inch, one heartbeat, from extinction. It's not a few seconds we spend there, it's our whole lives.

King Lear is not history, it's myth; but it tells profound truths about the workings of power and love. It does the artist's work of turning history inside out and telling us what's under the skin. Despite what Marx said, I don't believe history ever repeats itself, either as tragedy or farce. I think it's a live show and you get one chance. Blink and you miss it. Only through art can you live it again.

And without art, what have you, to inform you about the past? What lies beyond is the unedited flicker of closed-circuit TV. This technology offers to capture the world without bias, without interpretation. The pictures help us count heads in a crowd. They can help us nail a lie, or spot a wanted man. Yet the images from the mechanical eye have a peculiar chill, because they show us helpless against fate – parched automatons, occupying space without commanding it.

Think of those pictures of Diana, twenty years ago, leaving the Paris Ritz through the service corridor – her retreating back, only minutes before her death. To these images you are history's lonely, appalled witness, the eternal bystander. No creative hand is at work – just life, mutely and stupidly recorded, shown to us when it's too late to act, too late to learn. If we told our histories in that mode we would despair. Though the images of Diana are banal, artless, that still doesn't guarantee their perfect truth. The inquest heard that they came from five banks of cameras that were not quite synchronised: so on that most unlucky night, there were five different time zones on offer in the Ritz Hotel.

Death is certain, the hour of death uncertain, and our precise position on our path towards it is not, even in retrospect, as easy to pinpoint as you would think. If we crave truth unmediated by art we are chasing a phantom. We need the commentator's craft, even to make sense of the news. We need historians, not to collect facts, but to help us pick a path through the facts, to meaning. We need fiction to remind us that the unknown and unknowable is real, and exerts its force.

Some writers and adaptors disclaim responsibility. They say the public wants escapism – so let's give them what they want. They cheat their audience as politicians cheat when they make uncosted pledges: the bill comes later, when we lose a grip on our own story, and fall into individual distress and political incoherence.

I have written a novel called *The Giant, O'Brien*, loosely based on the true story of a real-life giant who came to London in the 1780s, to exhibit himself for money. In my version, the giant is more than a freakishly tall man: he is the embodiment and carrier of myth, and he has a fund of stories about love and war and talking animals and saints. His followers join in, shouting up with jokes and plot twists of their own. He tries to incorporate them and keep everybody happy. So his stories are interactive, democratic and popular – the only trouble is, they are corrupt. They get further and further from the story as he knows it to be.

In the end, he realises the folly of telling people what they want to hear. He says, 'Stories cannot save us . . . Unless we plead on our knees with history we are done for, we are lost.' History, of course, hears no plea: it is a human being who hears, the bearer of the tale. The giant's plea is for art and craft honestly deployed. Our audiences do not need to be protected from stories; they know when they enter the fictional space.

But we owe it to them to stretch our technique to offer the truth, in its multiple and layered forms – not to mislead because it is, on the face of it, the easier option – we should not avoid the complexities and contradictions of history, any more than politicians should abandon debate and govern by slogans. We must try by all the means we command to do justice to the past in its nuance, intricacy, familiarity and strangeness. Historical fiction acts to make the past a shared imaginative resource. It is more than a project of preservation: it is a project against death.

In the epigraph to my novel about the Irish giant, I quoted the poet George MacBeth, and I leave you with his thought about what we want from the past and how we get it:

> All crib from skulls and bones who push the pen.
> Readers crave bodies: we're the resurrection men.

2011

Eliza Manningham-Buller

Securing Freedom

Extract from 'Freedom'

Baroness Eliza Manningham-Buller (born 1948), is a retired British intelligence officer, formerly Director General of MI5 from 2002 to 2007. She was a joint Reith lecturer in 2011 with Aung San Suu Kyi, both sharing their thoughts on the theme of freedom. Manningham-Buller's series discussed policy priorities since 9/11. In her final lecture, she reflects on the Arab Spring and argues that the West's support of authoritarian regimes did, to some extent, fuel the growth of al-Qaeda; considering when we should talk to 'terrorists'.

I want to consider the wider policy context of terrorism. I do not do so as an expert in foreign or domestic policy, but as a retired security intelligence officer. In this lecture I want to argue that states should, wherever possible, seek political solutions and reconciliation. Secondly, that how a nation conducts its foreign policy has a direct bearing on its chances of success in the search for conciliation. And finally, I want to consider how our handling of risk, and the laws we pass to deal with it, can distort our response to the threat of terrorism.

In al-Qaeda we see a terrorist grouping with, in many ways, a medieval ideology, employing today's technology to great advantage. It works in a thoroughly modern way, virtual, amorphous, franchised and unbounded by geography. It has recruited people from all over the world. It understands the power of images, both in its campaign of terror and in its recruitment and proselytising material. It skilfully exploits the instant communications and social networking of the IT age. I think it also understands some of the vulnerability of the West: its appetite for news, its short-termism, its instant judgments and the pressures on its governments to respond to terrorism and the limited options open to them.

When I joined the security service, there was no internet,

international travel was expensive, there was less migration, borders were not generally porous and communications were usually by a fixed line telephone or a letter. I can remember special kettles being kept for steaming open letters. That will no longer suffice. The democratic state can no longer rely on its old tools to collect the intelligence it needs to protect itself. It will always wish to recruit human sources to provide inside information, but it also needs, subject to proper controls, oversight and legal safeguards, to try to redress the balance by using the latest powerful technologies to react quickly and to keep it one step ahead. The terrorist now has at his disposal tools which were once the sole preserve of the state. He has more advanced means of conspiring, mobilising and causing death and damage. So what is ethical, necessary and proportionate for the state to do in response cannot be set in stone.

I have known throughout my career that, however professional security and intelligence agencies working with the police may be, and whatever success they may have in preventing terrorist crimes, they can't stop everything. Similarly, however resourceful the terrorists may be, they will suffer attrition, betrayal, arrest and imprisonment as well as death.

Success for us will not be the absence of terror but less of it, with fewer deaths and a dwindling supply of new recruits. And that success is not likely to come from military effort or from security, intelligence and police work alone, but from long-term political and economic initiatives aimed at reducing the causes of terrorism and countering the extreme ideology in order to seek the peace and reconciliation that has been so striking in South Africa. Conciliation is never easy, sometimes impossible, but it's always worth trying. Security and intelligence work can play a valuable role in creating space for the political process which is central to that, but it cannot replace it.

So what might these political initiatives be? Some of the answers may be found in the Arab Spring. This year, triggered by the self-immolation of a Tunisian street trader, we've seen people in North Africa and the Middle East take to the streets – and sometimes to arms – in protest at the conditions under which they live. The list is long: Tunisia, Algeria, Lebanon, Jordan, Sudan, Oman, Saudi Arabia, Egypt, Syria, Morocco, Yemen, Bahrain, Kuwait and of course Libya.

Conditions in these countries obviously vary but the protesters have one thing in common, simply stated by one of the leaders of the Syrian protesters: 'We want what you have – freedom.' They are protesting in many cases at venal dictators, at absolute monarchs, at lack of human rights, at lack of freedom and association. They also, of course, want jobs, houses and education, and some share of the material wealth, which, where it exists, is too often monopolised by their rulers. Their passion for freedom shines out, encouraged by the visibility offered by the internet and promoted by social networks. They are prepared to risk their lives for the freedom we enjoy. The Arab Spring raises serious questions about al-Qaeda's relevance. It has not been able to respond convincingly to the widespread demand for change, despite its adroit use of technology and the media. Al-Qaeda's version of the ideal Islamic government seems to have had little appeal.

The Arab Spring also conclusively shows the hollowness of the cynical comments I have too often heard, that people elsewhere do not want democracy, and with no tradition of it, would not know how to practise it. There were similar patronising comments made about the countries of Eastern Europe when the Soviet Empire broke up and the Berlin Wall came down. There is also, among some, an assumption that any government replacing a dictatorship will become corrupt and unstable, subject to malign influences. But the fact that democracy often has a tough birth means that we should offer support where that is practical.

Our foreign policy must never forget that desire for freedom. It must encourage it, both to meet the wishes of those who lack it and for our own long-term self-interest. Perhaps inevitably short-term interests will intrude. Every now and again, governments assert the need for an ethical foreign policy. That laudable aim usually bumps up against the reality that many countries of the world are led by unscrupulous autocrats who use every means to hold on to power. They have little concern for the people they govern and often maintain power only by imprisoning their opponents and bribing their armed forces. Several of these countries are vital to our economic and security interests. Unfortunately there is no point talking only to our friends and allies. The world is a messy place and we need to engage with the people in power.

From my own perspective in the security service, I know that protecting British citizens would be impossible if we were restricted to talking to those whose values we share. I can remember plots to attack us, for example, with links to Indonesia, Somalia, the Philippines, Kenya, Algeria, Jordan and, of course, most importantly, Pakistan. That list is not comprehensive. We cannot just talk to the Swiss however enjoyable and easy that might be.

So what then of the contentious rapprochement with Gaddafi in 2003? I do not think that it was wrong in principle. The prize was his abandonment of his programme for nuclear and chemical weapons. Gaddafi is the man, as I know from personal experience, who supplied explosives, arms and cash to the Provisional IRA, indirectly causing the deaths of many of the victims of Irish terrorism, as well as being responsible himself for a whole series of atrocities. They included the murder of the London police officer Yvonne Fletcher and, notably, Lockerbie.

That small Scottish town was somewhere I lived for several weeks, as we and the police tried to piece together what had happened and start the search to find the culprits. The people of Lockerbie provided us with generous helpings of home-made food as we began the slow and painful investigation to understand why and how 270 people, mainly American students flying home for Christmas, had met their death, and to work towards a prosecution of those responsible. I can still see the ashen faces of young service personnel and police officers as they returned to the school, the temporary police headquarters, after long days searching for body parts and wreckage strewn over a vast area. Gaddafi's was a brutal regime and his own people suffered most of all.

Nevertheless, in 2003 the government made the difficult, but, I think, right decision to open talks. Had Gaddafi made progress with his nuclear and other programmes, he could still be in power today and threatening us. There are clearly questions to be answered about the various relationships that developed afterwards and whether the UK supped with a sufficiently long spoon. I cannot say more. I expect the Gibson Inquiry will address these issues.

It is right to use all our diplomatic efforts to encourage dictators to grant their people freedom. For we can surely recognise that participation in government, the belief at least that you can have some say, however slight, in how you are governed, that people's lives can be improved and their rights protected, reduces the need for terrorism.

Look at Northern Ireland, where former terrorists are in government. We should welcome this, not damn it. Look at many of our former colonies, whose first leaders had been imprisoned by us for terrorism. Look at Mandela and the ANC which used terror tactics when it was in exile.

In Northern Ireland, the Provisional IRA decided – partly as a result of intelligence successes against them – that pursuing a parallel policy of terrorism and politics, the armalite and the ballot box, was out-dated and it dropped the gun. The gradual move from terrorism into government is a long-established pattern. I hope that the greater freedom which should flow from the Arab Spring will undermine the attraction of the al-Qaeda narrative. If you are able to engage in your own political process, you have less cause to attack what across the Arab world is often called the 'Great Satan'.

Dialogue, not only with the dictators of the world but with the terrorists, is necessary. As Churchill said in the White House in 1954, 'To jaw-jaw is always better than to war-war.' Intelligence plays an important part and is of most value if working as part of a wider dialogue involving politics, diplomacy and economic process. My most relevant experience of this is the complex and prolonged talks in Northern Ireland. There are plenty of other examples, talking to Hezbollah, to Hamas.

Talking doesn't mean approval. It means an attempt to reduce the threat by addressing, if possible, its causes. It is a way of exploring peaceful options, of probing possibilities, of identifying whether there is room to manoeuvre, and what compromises, if any, may be reached, what political grievances can be acknowledged or even, in rare cases, accommodated. It is also the opportunity for governments to express their own positions. It requires courage by governments and a willingness to embark on an uncertain and tricky course which may well prove fruitless.

Not all terrorists are evil although their acts are. Nor are they all pathologically violent. A few are but many are not and have their own rationale, not ours, for what they do. In 1994 it was clear that the Provisional IRA was ready to move to proper talks with the British government about the future of Northern Ireland, but, misguidedly, they wished to do so from what they saw as a position of strength. So, shortly before talks were due to start, they dispatched to England a vast bomb concealed in the flat bed of a lorry. It was intercepted and defused, but had it exploded, say in the centre of London, it would have been politically impossible for the government to enter talks, and the peace process would have been further delayed. The Provisional IRA and its political wing, Sinn Fein, learned greater political sophistication through subsequent engagement.

And what about al-Qaeda? How might we talk to it? And do we even need to? It is not yet clear whether the death of Bin Laden has made the world a safer place and whether al-Qaeda has been permanently weakened. The Americans believe, and I obviously have no inside knowledge, that he remained the substantive leader of a dispersed organisation, the spider at the middle of the web, and that his death will reduce the amount of al-Qaeda terrorism we see. I hope they may be right, but webs are resilient and I doubt that his death will be a fatal blow to the organisation he founded or to the ideology he helped to create.

So what is there to discuss, what to negotiate about, what to agree on? Would any concessions be feasible? I don't know the answers to these questions, but I very much hope that there are those in the West who are exploring them. We are, after all, talking to the Taliban and may make progress.

Al-Qaeda is not a disciplined organisation with a clear structure. There will be those in al-Qaeda, or associated with its franchises, who are tired and disenchanted, for whom the violence has become sterile and sickening. Some, thwarted by lack of success, will be looking for a way out. There are already those prepared to help the West. Bearing in mind that we are judged by our deeds, we should also be capable of countering the credibility of the al-Qaeda narrative – that Islam is under attack from the West.

So we should try to reduce terrorism by talking to its advocates and practitioners and try to promote freedom through talking to dictators. But we should never forget who and what they are. We need to avoid helping dictators to survive. The West's record on that is poor. We have too often preferred the stability of the devil we know to the uncertainties of democracy. We cannot expect people round the world to fail to notice our hypocrisy if a gap exists between our professed support for freedom and our actions. People suffering from oppressive governments are bemused when the West talks of freedom and democracy while at the same time supporting regimes that deny them. Of course there may often be much going on behind the scenes and it's important to recognise the real value of quiet diplomacy and private pressure away from the glare of public criticism.

If we ourselves are to be free, and to feel secure in our free-dom, it's important to keep a rational perspective on terrorist risk. Bin Laden must have known that 9/11 would make this especially difficult, for at least two reasons: the endless images of the horror, recycled and replayed round the clock by the twenty-four-hour media, and the unrealistic view that society can become risk free. The world is full of risks and dangers, only some of which can be reduced.

Why then, when we in this country know that, for exam-ple, hospital-acquired infections and road traffic accidents both kill many more than terrorism, do we react as we do? The threat of violent death is potent. It can create commu-nity tension, including irrational Islamophobia, and cause loss of confidence in government, as in Spain after the train bombings in Madrid in 2004. It also places on government the tough dilemma of providing an authoritative response without giving the terrorists the status they seek.

One of the fears since 9/11 is that it or something similar could happen again. And of course it still could, although I would hope that the substantial investment in security and intelligence in the last ten years has made it less likely. It nearly happened with the plot to bring down up to a dozen transatlantic aircraft in 2006. Had that occurred, the death toll would have been very high, the economic cost enormous and the long-term effect frightening.

I mentioned in my second lecture that, while it was gov-ernment's responsibility to do what it could to protect its citizens from threats, governments should never imply that they were able to do so fully. Politicians lose their way if they become too apprehensive about how the media will react to terrorism when it happens. It is very difficult for governments to manage both economies that are shaken by terrorism and anxious public opinion. There are no military or security options that are certain of success.

Not all security risks, such as that from a xenophobic, right-wing Norwegian who appears to have acted alone, can be anticipated and countered. Moreover, political and media pressure to 'do something' in response to such events can lead to unnecessary, even counter-productive initiatives and new laws, which may offer false assurance that they will prevent the recurrence of the event which triggered them.

This is not a new phenomenon. When the security service was focused on Irish-related terrorism, it became used to being asked for suggestions for new legislation. There have been times when the service has argued strongly for legis-lation, for example for that governing its functions and its powers. But it has rarely argued for substantial counter-terror-ist powers, believing the criminal law to be broadly adequate.

Certainly rushing to legislate in the wake of a terrorist atrocity is often a mistake. It may be a well-intentioned mistake, designed to make us safer, but it would be better to reflect on the long-term wisdom of what may look immediately appealing. Since 9/11 there has been a slew of counter-terrorist legislation, some of it helpful, some of it justified as exceptional, partly because of the 'War on Terror' language. Quite rightly it has been scrutinised by parliament and the courts and some of it amended. Laws which involve reducing people's rights can themselves frighten the public. 'Should I be afraid,' the citizen asks, 'if the government feels these measures are necessary?'

What terrorism does is frighten us through its random effect and deter us from behaving normally. But we compound the problem of terrorism if we use it as a reason to erode the freedom of us all. That is why I spoke out against the proposal to detain terrorists without charge for up to forty-two days (ninety had been originally proposed). We were to give up something of value, in effect the principle of habeas corpus, and for what? Some greater spurious security? We must recognise the limits of what any government can do and be deeply cautious of anything that leads to security being seen as the opposite of liberty rather than essential to it. Governments should aim to limit and reduce the threat of terrorism, encourage its causes to be recognised and addressed, protect what it can, and be ready to react with calm when it happens, reasserting our belief in our freedoms and the rule of law.

And, as I hope I have made clear in this talk, governments need to practise a foreign policy that, while acknowledging the world as it is, tries to secure freedom for others – and to pursue a domestic policy that protects the liberties we value and which the terrorist tries to destroy.

2010

Martin Rees

Scientific Horizons

Extract from 'The Scientific Citizen'

Baron Martin Rees (born 1942), is a British cosmologist and astrophysicist, notable for his role as the Astronomer Royal and formerly as president of the Royal Society. His lecture series explored the challenges facing science in the twenty-first century. In his first lecture, Rees asks who we should trust to explain the risks we face.

I'll start with a flashback to the 1660s – to the earliest days of the Royal Society. Christopher Wren, Robert Hooke, Samuel Pepys, and other 'ingenious and curious gentlemen' (as they described themselves) met regularly. Their motto was to accept nothing on authority. They did experiments; they peered through newly invented telescopes and microscopes; they dissected weird animals. But, as well as indulging their curiosity, they were immersed in the practical agenda of their era – improving navigation, exploring the New World, and rebuilding London after the Great Fire.

Today, science has transformed our lives. Our horizons have hugely expanded; no new continents remain to be discovered. Our Earth no longer offers an open frontier, but seems constricted and crowded – a 'pale blue dot' in the immense cosmos.

My theme in these lectures is that the Royal Society's old values should endure. Today's scientists, like their forebears, probe nature and nature's laws by observation and experiment. But they should also engage broadly with society and with public affairs.

Indeed, their engagement is needed now more than ever. Science isn't just for scientists. All should have a voice in ensuring that it's applied optimally – and to the benefit of both the developing and developed world. We must confront widely held anxieties that genetics, brain science and artificial intelligence may 'run away' too fast. As citizens, we all need a feel for how much confidence can be placed in science's claims. This is a crucial century. The Earth has existed for 45 million centuries. But this is the first when one species, ours, can determine – for good or ill – the future of the entire biosphere.

But first, a comment on how science itself has changed our perspective on nature.

Last year, we celebrated Charles Darwin's anniversary. Darwin's impact on Victorian thought was profound – and he resonates even more today. His concept of natural selection has been described, with only slight hyperbole, as 'the best idea anyone ever had'. His insights are pivotal to our understanding of all life on Earth, and the vulnerability of our environment to human actions. Other sciences have disclosed the nature of atoms, of DNA, and of stars. Spectacular images from space have enlarged our cosmic horizons.

It's a cultural deprivation not to appreciate the panorama offered by modern cosmology and Darwinian evolution – the chain of emergent complexity leading from some still-mysterious beginning to atoms, stars and planets. And how on our planet, life emerged, and evolved into a biosphere containing creatures with brains able to ponder the wonder

47

of it all. This common understanding should transcend all national differences – and all faiths too.

Science is indeed a global culture, and its universality is specially compelling in my own subject of astronomy. The dark night sky is an inheritance we've shared with all humanity, throughout history. All have gazed up in wonder at the same 'vault of heaven', but interpreted it in diverse ways.

I'm not going to speak further about the findings of science, nor will I extol it as the greatest collective achievement of humanity – though it surely is. I'll instead focus on how it impinges on our lives – and how it will in future.

Some changes happen with staggering speed. Everyday life has been transformed in less than two decades by mobile phones and the internet. Computers double their power every two years. Spin-offs from genetics could soon be as pervasive as those from the microchip have already been. Ten years ago, the first draft of the human genome was decoded. Now, genome sequencing – the 'read-out' of our genetic inheritance – is a million times cheaper than ten years ago.

These rapid advances – and others across the whole of science – raise profound questions.

For instance:

Who should access the 'read-out' of our personal genetic code?

How will our lengthening life-spans affect society?

Should we build nuclear power stations – or windmills – if we want to keep the lights on?

Should we use more insecticides or plant GM crops?

How much should computers invade our privacy?

Such questions didn't feature much in the recent election campaign here in the UK. That's partly because they transcend party politics. But it's more because they are long-term – and tend to be trumped by more urgent items on political agendas.

But often science does have an *urgent* impact on our lives. Governments and businesses, as well as individuals, then need advice – advice that fairly presents the level of confidence, and the degree of uncertainty.

Issues come up unexpectedly. For instance, back in April, the eruption in Iceland raised urgent questions about vulcanology; about wind patterns, and about how volcanic dust affects jet engines. In that instance, the knowledge was basically there: what was lacking was coordination, and an agreement on the acceptable level of risk.

Sometimes, though, the key science *isn't* known. An example was the outbreak of 'mad cow disease' in the 1980s. At first, experts conjectured that this disease posed no threat to humans because it resembled scrapie in sheep, which had been endemic for 200 years without crossing the species barrier. That was a reasonable conjecture, and comforting to politicians and public. But it proved wrong. The pendulum then swung the other way. Banning 'beef on the bone', for instance, was in retrospect an over-reaction, but at the time seemed a prudent precaution against a potential tragedy that could have been far more widespread than it actually turned out to be.

Likewise, the government could have been right to stock up vaccine against swine flu – even though, fortunately, this particular epidemic proved milder than feared.

Indeed, if we apply to pandemics the same prudent analysis whereby we calculate an insurance premium – multiplying probability by consequences – we'd surely conclude that measures to alleviate this kind of extreme event actually need scaling up.

Incidentally, there's a mismatch between public perception of very different risks and their actual seriousness. We fret unduly about carcinogens in food and low-level radiation. But we are in denial about 'low-probability high consequence' events which should concern us more. The recent financial crash was one such; but others that haven't yet happened – lethal pandemics are one example – should loom higher on the agenda.

The varied topics I've just mentioned show how pervasive science is, in our lives and in public policy.

President Obama certainly recognised this. He filled some key posts in his administration with a real 'dream team' of top-rate scientists. And he opined that their advice should be heeded, I quote, 'even when it is inconvenient – indeed *especially* when it is inconvenient.'

The UK has 'chief science advisors' in most government departments. Not yet, however, in the Treasury – though I can't help thinking this would be worthwhile, even at the sacrifice of one economist.

Winston Churchill once said that scientists should be 'on tap, not on top'. And it is indeed the elected politicians who should make decisions. But the role of scientific advice is not just to provide facts to support policies. Experts should be prepared to challenge decision-makers, and help them navigate the uncertainties of science. But there's one thing they mustn't forget. Whether the context be nuclear power, drug classification, or health risks, political decisions are seldom *purely* scientific. They involve ethics, economics and social policies as well. And in domains beyond their special expertise, scientists speak just as citizens.

There's no denying where science has recently had the most contentious policy impact, and where the stakes are highest: climate change.

It will feature, along with other global threats, in my second lecture, but I'll venture some comments today too. As regards the science, there is, in my inexpert view, one decisive measurement: the amount of carbon dioxide in the atmosphere is higher than it's been for a million years, and is rising, mainly because of the burning of fossil fuels. This finding isn't controversial. And straightforward chemistry tells us that carbon dioxide is a so-called 'greenhouse gas': it acts like a blanket, preventing some of the heat radiated by the Earth from escaping freely into space. So the measured carbon dioxide build-up in the atmosphere will trigger a long-term warming, superimposed on all the other complicated effects that make climate fluctuate.

The predicted rate of warming, however, is uncertain – depending on the poorly-understood 'feedback' from water vapour and clouds, which themselves affect the blanketing. Nevertheless, even the existing uncertain science convinces me that the threat of disruptive climate change is serious enough to justify its priority on the agenda of this country and others.

This confidence may surprise anyone who has dipped into all that's been written on the subject. Any trawl of the internet reveals diverse and contradictory claims. So how do you make up your mind? I'd suggest the following analogy.

Suppose you seek medical guidance. Googling any ailment reveals a bewildering range of purported remedies. But if your own health were at stake, you wouldn't attach equal weight to everything in the blogosphere: you'd entrust your diagnosis to someone with manifest medical credentials. Likewise, we get a clearer 'steer' on climate by attaching more weight to those with a serious record in the subject.

But – as I said earlier about science advice in general – it's crucial to keep 'clear water' between the science on the one hand, and the policy response on the other. Risk assessment should be separate from risk management.

Climate projections still span a wide range, but even if

there were minimal uncertainties in how the world's weather might change, there would still be divergent views on what governments should do about it.

For instance, what balance should be struck between mitigating climate change and adapting to it? How much should we sacrifice now to ensure that the world is no worse when our grandchildren grow old? How much should we incentivise clean energy?

On all these choices, there's as yet minimal consensus, still less effective action. But policies, and investment priorities, are being influenced by climate change projections. So it's inevitable, and right, that climate science is under specially close scrutiny.

We are today far more questioning of authorities on every topic. We can all access far more information and want to weigh up evidence for ourselves. Such scrutiny should be welcome: just as there are instances of shoddy work, error or even malpractice in the medical and legal profession, so there occasionally are in science.

But science is generally 'self-correcting'. Scientists are their own severest critics. They have more incentive than anyone else to uncover errors. That's because the greatest esteem goes to those who contribute something unexpected and original – like refuting a consensus. That's how in science initially-tentative ideas firm up – not only on climate change, but – to take earlier examples – regarding the link between smoking and lung cancer, and between HIV and AIDS. But that's also how seductive theories get destroyed by harsh facts. Science is 'organised scepticism'. Our scientific knowledge and capability is actually surprisingly patchy. Odd though it may seem, some of the best-understood phenomena are far away in the cosmos. Right back in the seventeenth century, Isaac Newton could describe the 'clockwork of the heavens' and predict eclipses. But few other things are so predictable. For instance, it's still hard to forecast, even a day before, whether those who go to view an eclipse will encounter clouds or clear skies. And guidance on some everyday matters – aspects of diet and child care for instance – still changes from year to year.

If you ask scientists what they are working on, you will seldom get an inspirational reply like 'seeking to cure cancer' or 'understanding the universe'. They focus on a tiny piece of the puzzle; they tackle something that seems tractable. They're not ducking the 'grand challenges' – but they're judging that an oblique approach can pay off best.

A frontal attack may be premature. For instance, forty years ago President Richard Nixon declared a 'war on cancer'. He envisaged this as a national goal, modelled on the then-recent Apollo moon-landing programme. But there was a crucial difference. The science underpinning Apollo was already understood. So, when funds gushed at NASA, it became reality. But in the case of cancer, the scientists knew too little to be able to target their efforts effectively.

By the way, I'm using the word 'science' throughout, in a

broad sense, to encompass technology and engineering – this is not just to save words, but because they're symbiotically linked. 'Problem solving' motivates us all – whether one is an astronomer probing the remote cosmos, or an engineer facing a down-to-earth design conundrum. There is at least as much challenge in the latter – a point neatly made by an old cartoon showing two beavers looking up at a hydroelectric dam. One beaver says, 'I didn't actually build it, but it's based on my idea.'

Nixon's cancer programme, incidentally, facilitated a lot of good research into genetics and the structure of cells. Indeed, the overall investment in scientific research in the twentieth century paid off abundantly. But the pay-off happens unpredictably, and after a time-lag that can be decades long. And that of course is why much of science has to be funded as a 'public good'.

A fine 'case study' is the laser, invented in 1960. It applied basic ideas that Einstein had developed more than forty years earlier. And its inventors in turn didn't foresee that lasers would be used in eye surgery and in DVD players.

Traditionally, discoveries reach public attention only after surviving peer review. But this 'copybook' procedure is under increasing strain, due to competitive or commercial pressures, twenty-four-hour media – and the greater scale and diversity of a scientific enterprise that's now widely international.

A conspicuous departure from traditional norms happened back in 1989 when Stanley Pons and Martin Fleischmann, then at the University of Utah, claimed at a press conference to have generated nuclear power using a tabletop apparatus. If credible, it would have ranked as one of the most momentous breakthroughs since the discovery of fire. But doubts set in. Extraordinary claims demand extraordinary evidence, and in this case the evidence proved far from robust. Others failed to reproduce what Pons and Fleischmann claimed they'd done. Within a year, there was a consensus that the results were misinterpreted, though even today a few believers remain.

'Cold fusion' bypassed the normal quality controls of the scientific profession, but it did no great harm in the long run. Indeed, in any similar episode today, exchanges via the internet would have led to a consensus verdict even more quickly. But this fiasco holds an important lesson: what's crucial in sifting error and validating scientific claims is open discussion. Suppose that Pons and Fleischmann had worked not in a university but in a lab whose mission was military, or commercially confidential. What would have happened then? If those in charge were convinced that they had stumbled on something stupendous, a massive programme might have got under way, shielded from open scrutiny and wasting huge resources.

The imperative for open-ness and debate is a common thread through all the examples I've discussed. It ensures that any scientific consensus that emerges is robust and firmly grounded. Even wider discussion is needed when what's in contention is not the science itself, but how new findings should be applied. Such discussions should engage all of us, as citizens – and of course our elected representations, not just the scientists.

Sometimes this has happened, and constructively too. In the UK, ongoing dialogue with parliamentarians led to a generally admired legal framework on embryos and stem cells – a contrast to what happened in the US. But we've had failures too: the GM crop debate was left too late – to a time when opinion was already polarised between eco-campaigners on the one side and commercial interests on the other.

But what about ideas 'beyond the fringe' – the illusory comfort and assurance of the pseudosciences? Here there is less scope for debate – both sides don't share the same methods or play by the same evidence-based rules. I've not found it fruitful to have much dialogue with astrologers or with creationists.

A word now about communicating science. I mentioned Darwin earlier. Back in 1860, his book *The Origin of Species* was a best seller: readily accessible – even fine literature – as well as an epochal contribution to science. What scientists today call 'the literature' isn't accessible in this way at all. But its essence can generally be conveyed, free of jargon and mathematics, by skilled communicators. Misperceptions about Darwin or dinosaurs are an intellectual loss, but no more. In the medical arena, however, they could be a matter of life and death. Hope can be cruelly raised by claims of miracle cures; exaggerated scares can distort healthcare choices, as happened over the MMR vaccine.

When reporting a particular viewpoint, journalists should clarify whether it is widely supported, or whether it is contested by 99 per cent of specialists. Noisy controversy need not signify evenly balanced arguments. Of course the establishment is sometimes routed and a maverick vindicated. We all enjoy seeing this happen – but such instances are rarer than is commonly supposed. Scientists should expect media scrutiny. Their expertise is crucial in areas that fascinate us, and matter to us all. And they shouldn't be bashful in proclaiming the overall promise that science offers.

I'll end, as I began, with a flashback – this time to the atomic scientists who developed the first nuclear weapons during World War II. Fate had assigned them a pivotal role in history. Many of them returned with relief to peacetime academic pursuits. But the ivory tower wasn't, for them, a sanctuary. They continued not just as scientists but as engaged citizens – promoting efforts to control the power they had helped unleash. These men – Joe Rotlat, Hans Bethe and the others – were an elite group. The alchemists of their time, possessors of secret knowledge.

The dominant issues today, in contrast, span all the sciences. They are far more open, and often global. There's less demarcation between experts and laypersons. Campaigners and bloggers enrich the debate. But professionals have special obligations to engage – the atomic scientists were fine exemplars. Scientists shouldn't be indifferent to the fruits of their ideas. They should try to foster benign spin-offs – commercial or otherwise. And they should resist, as far as they can, dubious or threatening applications. Unprecedented pressures confront the world, but there are unprecedented prospects too. The benefits of globalisation must be fairly shared.

There's a widening gap between what science allows us to do and what it's prudent or ethical actually to do – there are doors that science could open but which are best left closed. Everyone should engage with these choices but their efforts must be leveraged by 'scientific citizens' – scientists from all fields of expertise – engaging, from all political perspectives, with the media, and with a public attuned to the scope and limit of science.

Jeffrey Sachs

Bursting at the Seams

Extract from 'Bursting at the Seams'

Jeffrey Sachs (born 1954), is an American economist, considered to be the leading international economic advisor of his generation. His Reith Lecture series set out a blueprint to help make globalisation work for all, considering the emergence of new economic superpowers and the challenges of extreme poverty against the need for international cooperation. In his first lecture, Sachs outlines the challenges facing mankind and argues that we must adapt to the new age.

I want to start with my favourite speech of the modern American presidency and, I think, one of the most important statements made in modern times, one that truly did change the course of history. I'm referring to John Kennedy's Commencement Address at American University, 10 June 1963. It was an address that helped rescue the world from a path of self-destruction. It came in the immediate wake of the Cuban missile crisis, when Kennedy and the world had peered over the abyss, and what President John Kennedy said on that day I think resonates today and is important for all of us in all parts of the world.

He said:

'First, examine our attitude towards peace itself. Too many of us think it is impossible, too many think it is unreal, but that is a dangerous, defeatist belief. It leads to the conclusion that war is inevitable, that mankind is doomed, that we are gripped by forces we cannot control. We need not accept that view. Our problems are man-made, therefore they can be solved by man, and man can be as big as he wants. No problem of human destiny is beyond human beings. Man's reason and spirit have often solved the seemingly unsolvable, and we believe they can do it again. I am not referring to the absolute infinite concept of universal peace and goodwill of which some fantasies and fanatics dream. I do not deny the value of hopes and dreams, but we merely invite discouragement and incredulity by making that our only and immediate goal.

'Let us focus instead on a more practical, more attainable peace, based not on a sudden revolution in human nature but on a gradual evolution in human institutions, on a series of concrete actions and effective agreements which are in the interest of all concerned. There is no single, simple key to this peace, no grand or magic formula to be adopted by one or two powers. Genuine peace must be the product of many nations, the sum of many acts. It must be dynamic, not static, changing to meet the challenge of each new generation, for peace is a process, a way of solving problems.'

I want to talk about the challenge of our generation. Ours is not the generation that faced the challenge of Fascism, ours is not the generation to have first grappled with the nuclear demon, though we still grapple with it today. Ours is not the generation that faced the Cold War. Ours is not the generation incidentally in which the greatest problem is the war on terror, or Iran, or other ideas that are current. Our challenge, our generation's unique challenge, is learning to live peacefully and sustainably in an extraordinarily crowded world.

Our planet is crowded to an unprecedented degree. It is bursting at the seams. It's bursting at the seams in human terms, in economic terms, and in ecological terms. This is our greatest challenge: learning to live in a crowded and inter-connected world that is creating unprecedented pressures on human society and on the physical environment. As John Kennedy said, we will need to solve these problems, the ones that are unique to our generation, if we are to find peace. Obviously we are not just in a cold war, we are in a hot war right now, because we have failed to understand the challenges and we have failed to take appropriate measures to face them. We don't need to dream. I am going to talk about concrete actions, I am going to discuss, I hope, effective agreements, and most importantly I want to talk about a way of solving problems. It's a fascinating and crucial concept for us – peace as a way of solving problems. We clearly are not on a path of problem solving now with the world, we are on a path of increasing risk and increasing instability, and by all objective measures the path of increasing hatred as well. We have not yet found a way of solving problems that our generation faces now.

Most importantly for us on this crowded planet, facing the challenges of living side by side as never before, and facing a common ecological challenge, has never been upon us in human history until now. The way of solving problems requires one fundamental change, a big one, and that is learning that the challenges of our generation are not us versus them, they are not us versus Islam, us versus the terrorists, us versus Iran, they are us, all of us together on this planet against a set of shared and increasingly urgent problems. By understanding those problems, understanding them at their depth, understanding what we share with every part of this world in the need to face these challenges, we can find peace. But we are living in a cloud of confusion, where we have been told that the greatest challenge on the planet is us versus them, a throwback to a tribalism that we must escape for our own survival.

I'm going to talk about three common problems that we face. They are interconnected, they build on each other in ways that amplify or create abrupt change, abrupt risk, and highly non-linear responses to the threats we face. The first challenge that I'll talk about is the challenge of what Paul Crutzen has magnificently called the Anthropocene. That is the idea that for the first time in history the physical systems of the planet – chemical fluxes, the climate, habitats, bio-diversity, evolutionary processes – are to an incredible and unrecognised extent under human forcings that now dominate a large measure of the most central ecological, chemical and biophysical processes on the planet – the hydrological cycle, the carbon cycle, the nitrogen cycle, the location and extinction of species, and basic physical habitats. Of course, human forcings have always played their role. We know that the hominids already controlled fire a million or more years ago, and therefore changed landscapes, even before the rise of homo sapiens. But never has the control of such fundamental processes been determined by human forcings, and we've barely awakened to that reality.

The second common challenge is a challenge of geo-politics, a challenge that I'm going to call the Age of Conver-gence. In many ways it's wonderful news. It's the notion that in a world that is more connected than ever before, a world where economic development, at least for the last two hun-dred and fifty years, has been driven by technology, and now a world where those technologies diffuse rapidly around the world, we have the fabulous prospect for the rapid closing of economic gaps that now exist between the rich and the poor. One result is that there will be in our time a fundamental shift of economic power, and the political power that goes along with it. We started this decade with a fantasy, the fantasy of the United States as the world's sole superpower, the fantasy of the United States as the sole indispensable power, it was called, the fantasy which we should have known from history always to be wrong and dangerous, of the United States as the New Rome, being urged on to take on the imperial mantle even by some who ought to know a lot better. But it was a fan-tasy because just as this was being proclaimed, China, India, and other regional powers were bound to be increasing their influence and their economic weight in the world by virtue of the shared capacity to benefit from technology, which is the foundation of economic development. As an economist, I subscribe to a philosophy that was first initiated by Adam Smith in 1776. Smith talked about how global markets and international trade can be a fundamental diffusion mechanism for these technologies, and now that is happening. But we're not ready for it.

I want to call the third of our common challenges the Challenge of the Weakest Links. In an interconnected world, all parts of the world are affected by what happens in all other parts of the world, and sometimes surprisingly so. We cannot be surprised when events in some far off and distant place – and I'm not talking about Central Europe, I'm talking about halfway around the world in the landmass of Eurasia – can be of fundamental significance even for survival, for the spending of hundreds of billions, if not trillions, of dollars for the direction of global politics. In an interconnected world we have great need and basic responsibility, for our own survival, to attend to the weakest links. By that I mean those places in the world that suffer, those places in the world where people die because they are too poor to stay alive, those parts of the world which – by virtue of physical geography, epidemiology, climate stress, rain-fed agriculture and drought-prone savannah climates, for example – face horrific challenges to even get onto the ladder of development. One billion people on the planet are too poor, too hungry, too disease-burdened, too bereft of the most basic infrastructure even to get on the ladder of development. The rich world seems to be believe, despite all the fine speeches (and there have been many), that this doesn't really matter, because the actions of the rich countries don't begin to address this problem. We are leaving ten million people to die every year because they are too poor to stay alive. Fine speeches will not solve that problem.

Our challenge is to understand these common problems, to see that the whole world is arrayed on the same side of them; to understand that a leader in Iran, or in Korea, or in Sudan, or in other places where we've made it a point not even to have a conversation, much less a negotiation or an attempt at peaceful solution, is facing problems of water supply, climate change, food production, poverty and disease burden, many of which impinge directly on us.

Can it be true incidentally that because we don't want to talk to Iran, H5N1 won't pass through Iran, that we won't have to deal with avian flu in places we don't want to speak to, where we have put pre-conditions to negotiations, because we can't see the commonality of our problems? Can it really be that the solution to Darfur, one of the most urgent crises on the planet, is all about peacekeepers and troops and sanctions, when we know that in Western Darfur the rebellion started because this is just about the poorest place on the whole planet, because there is not enough water to keep people alive, the livestock have no veterinary care, there's no basic infrastructure, and the electricity grid is hundreds of miles away? Can we really think that peacekeeping troops and sanctions will solve this problem? I do think we have a fundamental rethinking to do in each of these areas.

I'll discuss the Anthropocene in Beijing, China, which soon will be the country that is the largest emitter of carbon dioxide on the planet, and one that faces its own profound challenges of water stress, which will worsen, perhaps immeasurably, as the glaciers of the Himalayas melt and as the seasonal timing of snow melt from the Himalayas changes the river flow of the Yangtze and Yellow rivers and other rivers of Asia. The Anthropocene tells us that it's not just about one problem, as Sir Nicholas Stern, one of the intellectual leaders of our time, has brilliantly exposed in his report for the UK government. It's not only the problem of mass extinctions, or only the problem of the mass destruction of fisheries in the North Atlantic and in many other parts of the world. We are weighing so heavily on the Earth's systems, not only through carbon dioxide emissions changing climate but through carbon dioxide emissions acidifying oceans, through destruction of habitat, which is literally driving perhaps millions of species right off the planet. We are over-hunting, over-fishing, and over-gathering just about anything that grows slowly or moves slowly. If we can catch it, we kill it. Our capacity in the Anthropocene is unprecedented, poorly understood, out of control, and a grave and common threat.

The illusions about geo-politics which I mentioned prevent us from solving these problems as well. The United States, my own country, has been in a fantasy of 'going it alone', when our problems are so fundamentally global and shared. How do you address climate change, even if you recognised it, by yourself? The US government solved that problem temporarily by not recognising it. But when they do recognise it they're going to have to recognise it in a shared and global way.

And how can it be that we think we can be safe? We think we can be safe when we leave a billion people to struggle literally for their daily survival, the poorest billion for whom every day is a fight to secure enough nutrients, a fight against the pathogen in the water that can kill them or their child, a fight against a mosquito bite carrying malaria or another killer disease for which no medicine is available, though the medicines exist and are low cost, thus letting malaria kill one or two million children this year. How can this be safe? How can we choose, as we do in the United States, to have a budget request this year of $623 billion for the military – more than all the rest of the world combined – and just $4.5 billion for all assistance to Africa and think that this is prudent? One might say it is science fiction that a zoonotic disease could arise and somehow spread throughout the world, except that AIDS is exactly that. How many examples do we need to understand the linkages, and the common threats, and the recklessness of leaving people to die – recklessness of spirit, of human heart, and of geo-political safety for us?

President Kennedy talked about a way of solving problems, and that too will be a theme of these lectures. We are entering, I believe, a new politics, and potentially a hopeful politics. I'm going to call it open-source leadership. If Wikipedia and Linux can be built in an open-source manner, politics can be done in that manner as well. We are going to need a new way to address and to solve global problems, but our connectivity will bring us tools unimaginable even just a few years ago. Without a global government we can still get global cooperation; initiatives like the Millennium Development Goals can be an organising principle for the world – though there is no single implementing authority – and it is possible to coalesce around shared goals. Scientists can play a fundamental role in this, such as they do in the Intergovernmental Panel on Climate Change (IPCC). The world is hungry for serious knowledge, for the information from what are sometimes called epistemic communities – that is communities of expertise – that can help to bring the best information to bear on the most crucial problems that affect the survival and the livelihoods and the well-being of people around the world.

Our governments can be reorganised and need to be reorganised because we are living with nineteenth and twentieth century government structures for twenty-first century problems. Our governments simply do not understand the nature of these problems. Ministries generally are like stove pipes, narrowly defined. That's often true in academia as well. The problems I am talking about cross disciplines and areas of knowledge, and inherently require cross-disciplinary and novel thinking, whether they are problems of poverty, disease, climate change, energy systems, war and peace, or Darfur. These problems cannot be left to the normal ways of operation, but that is what we are doing. That is why we see our governments flailing about blindly. These are not just 'intelligence' failures, in the sense of our spy agencies, though surely those exist and are serious. We are experiencing the deep incapacities of our government to understand these challenges. We need some fundamental reorganisation.

We need, as President Kennedy said, concrete actions. There is no sense in theory if there is not something to do, starting today. There are things to do in all of these areas that can make a difference, a life and death difference. We need – this is the possibility of our interconnected, socially networked internet-empowered age – involvement from all of us. We all play a role. It doesn't just go through government, and if government remains as impervious to evidence and knowledge and capacity as it is right now, we're going to have to go increasingly around government. Perhaps that's inevitable, perhaps that's just a particular failing of our immediate times, I'm not sure. But we are going to have to play unique roles in terms of corporate social responsibility, civil society, and as individuals as well.

I'm an optimist, though you might not detect it! I want you to sit up, with open eyes. You know many or all of the things I'm saying, and certainly if there is one introductory note it is that we must not for one moment think that we're on an acceptable course right now. I want to stress, however, that fundamentally we have choices, and we actually have some terrific choices. We have the ability to do things at much lower cost, and much greater efficacy, than almost any of us can know, unless we are lucky enough to be engaged in epistemic communities that allow us to hear the wonderful news.

I'm a partisan, for example, of anti-malaria bed nets, and I'll just give you one fact. There are three hundred million sleeping sites in Africa that need protection from malaria. Anti-malaria bed nets last five years, and cost a mere five dollars – one dollar per year. Often more than one child sleeps under a net. Economists are reasonably good at multiplication, so for three hundred million sleeping sites at five dollars per net, I calculate $1.5 billion. I also am acceptably good at long division. $620 billion of military budget, divided by 365 days, tells me that we are now spending $1.7 billion per day on the Pentagon. John Kennedy said in his world changing speech, 'for we are both devoting massive sums of money to weapons that could be better devoted to combat ignorance, poverty and disease,' and my little calculation has shown you that one day's Pentagon spending could cover every sleeping site in Africa for five years with anti-malaria bed nets. And yet we have not found our way to that bargain, the most amazing one of our time. We do have choices – they are good ones if we take them.

I want to close with what President Kennedy said about that. I regard these among the most beautiful lines ever uttered by a world leader. First he said, 'In short, both the United States and its allies, and the Soviet Union and its allies, have a mutually deep interest in a just and genuine peace, and in halting the arms race. Agreements to this end are in the interests of the Soviet Union as well as ours, and even the most hostile nations can be relied upon to accept and to keep those treaty obligations, and only those treaty obligations, which are in their own interest.' He uttered those words and within a few weeks the limited test ban treaty was negotiated. He changed the course of history by showing that there was a path for peace that was mutually acceptable. But then he said this, and what could be more important for the challenges of our generation?

So let us not be blind to our differences, but let us also direct attention to our common interests, and the means by which those differences can be resolved. And if we cannot end now our differences, at least we can help make the world safe for diversity, for in the final analysis our most basic common link is that we all inhabit this small planet, we all breathe the same air, we all cherish our children's future, and we are all mortal.

2006

Daniel Barenboim

⌣

In the Beginning was Sound

Extract from 'The Neglected Sense'

Daniel Barenboim (born 1942), is a world-leading musi-
cian and conductor, known as the most versatile pianist
of his generation. His Reith Lecture series examined the
interplay between music and society. In this, his second
lecture, Barenboim argued that we rarely listen to the
music of our choosing and that too often we hear music
which we have no control over. He put forward the case
that this unwelcome 'muzak' is largely responsible for
encouraging people not just to neglect the ear but to
repress it.

If St John said 'In the beginning there was the word', and Goethe says 'In the beginning there was the deed', I would like to examine this a little bit, saying, 'In the beginning there was sound', and for that it is important to dwell on the very simple fact that sound is perceived by the ear.

The ear is probably the most intelligent organ the body has. It is not for nothing that Aristotle said that 'the eyes are the organs of temptation, and the ears are the organs of instruction', because the ear does not only take sound or noise in, but by sending it directly to the brain, it sets into motion the whole creative process of thought that the human being is capable of.

The first quality that comes to my mind as to the intelligence of the ear is that the ear helps us tremendously to remember and to recollect, and the ear is therefore the basis for all the aspects that have to do with music-making, both for the performer and for the listener. The ear remembers, the ear recollects, and that shows you one of the most important elements of expression in music, one of repetition and accumulation. This goes into many areas, and composers have achieved great mastery of all the repeating – sometimes short parts of a theme, or of a motif – and creating different kinds of accumulation. The ear has this incredible memory.

The ear, let us not forget, starts operating on the forty-fifth day of the pregnancy of a woman. That means the foetus that is in the womb of a pregnant lady begins to use his ear on the forty-fifth day of the pregnancy, which means it has seven and a half months' advance over the eye. Therefore the question is, what do we in our society, in our civilisation, do to continue this process and this wonderful fact that we have seven and a half months' advantage?

Wagner understood the phenomenon of sound and the phenomenology of sound so well that he created a theatre, Festspielhaus in Bayreuth, where the pit is covered. Now at first sight most people think Wagner wrote so loud for the orchestra, if you cover the pit then the singers will be heard. But I think this is very basic, and evident. The mystery of Bayreuth is especially evidenced when the opera starts softly. You don't know when the sound is going to start, nor where does it come from. And therefore the ear is doubly alert, and the eye has to wait until the curtain goes up, whereas the ear has already prepared you for the whole drama.

This is linked to Wagner's whole idea about opera. After all, overtures to operas before Wagner very often were just brilliant pieces that were meant to make the public sit and be ready. The 'Marriage of Figaro' overture has actually nothing to do with the piece, and I wonder if one could not play the overture to 'Cosi Fan Tutte' instead. This is no criticism of either, but there is very little connection except that they both are there to make people sit up and listen. Wagner, who was more systematic, more, shall we say, Teutonic in his thinking, in the same way he was about everything including his anti-Semitism, he thought that the ear hears the overture, and it not only puts you in the mood but also tells part of the story.

The audience is inextricably linked to the very essence of the drama. And therefore the ear plays the role of the guide in the museum. We don't have an oral guide, we have to provide it ourselves: one reason why active listening is absolutely essential. But there are some things about the ear which we know; which it may not be out of place to remind ourselves of here. One is that it depicts physical vibrations and converts them into signals which become sound sensations, or auditory images in the brain; and, that the space occupied by the auditory system in the brain is smaller than the space occupied by the visual system; and, that the eye detects patterns of light and converts them into signals which become visual images in the brain. All this is common knowledge.

The well-known neurobiologist and neuroscientist Antonio Damasio has taught us many things about human emotion, about the human brain, and also about the human ear. He says that the auditory system is physically much closer inside the brain to the parts of the brain which regulate life, which means that they are the basis for the sense of pain, pleasure, motivation – in other words basic emotions. He also says that the physical vibrations which result in sound sensations are a variation on touching; they change our own bodies directly and deeply, more so than the patterns of light that lead to vision, because the patterns of light that lead to vision allow us to see objects sometimes very far away, provided there is light, but sound *penetrates* our body. There is no penetration, if you want, physical penetration, with the eye, but there is with the ear.

When a baby is born, in many cases – in fact in most cases – the ear is totally neglected. Everything is centred on the eye. The fact that we live in a primarily visual society comes much later. Already in infancy the child is more often than not made more and more aware of what he sees and not about what he hears. It is also, let's face it, a means of survival. When you take a small child to teach him how to cross the street, what do you say? Look to the right, look to the left, see that no cars are coming otherwise you will be run over. Therefore you depend on your eyes for survival. The ear is very often neglected.

I find much that is to my ears insensitive or disturbing goes totally unnoticed by society, starting with the coughing in the concert – as my friend and colleague Alfred Brendel has often remarked in great detail – to many other noises to which we are totally insensitive. The equivalent of that to the eye would be enough reason I think to find it so offensive that people could even be accused of disturbing society. Just think of the most despicable aspect of pornography and how offensive that is. There are many things which are just as disturbing for the ear which are not really taken into consideration.

Not only do we neglect the ear but we often repress it. We find more and more in our society, not only in the United States, although the United States I think was very active in starting this process, we are creating opportunities to hear music without listening to it – what is commonly known as muzak. I have spent many very happy years in the US, but I have suffered tremendously. In the hotel where I stay they think that it is very culturally minded to play classical music in the elevator, or in the foyers of concert halls before the concert. I have been on more than one occasion subject to having to hear, because I cannot shut my ears, the Brahms violin concerto in the lift, then having to conduct it in the evening. And I ask myself, why? This is not going to bring one more person into the concert hall. It is not only counter-productive but I think, if we are allowed an old term to speak of musical ethics, it is absolutely offensive.

The most extraordinary example of offensive usage of music, because it underlines some kind of association which I fail to recognise, was shown to me one day when watching the television in Chicago and seeing a commercial of a company called American Standard. It showed a plumber running very very fast in great agitation, opening the door to a toilet and showing why this company actually cleans the toilet better than other companies. And you know what music was played to that? The 'Lachrymose' from Mozart's *Requiem*.

I'm probably immodest enough to think I have a sense of humour but I can't laugh at this. I laughed even less when

I read this letter published, I'm afraid I don't know in what newspaper, sent in by Christine Statmuller of Basking Ridge. It is in reference to her previous letter which ran in the April issue of *The Catholic Spirit*.

'Thanks for printing my letter in which I objected to the use of music from Mozart's *Requiem* by American Standard to advertise their new champion toilet. As you can see from the enclosed letter below, it achieved results, thanks to the letters from other incensed readers.'

And the letter is as follows:

'Thank you for contacting American Standard with your concerns about the background music in the current television commercial for our champion toilet. We appreciate that you have taken the time to communicate with us, and share your feelings on a matter that clearly is very important to you. When we first selected Mozart's *Requiem*, we didn't know of its religious significance. We actually learned about it from a small number of customers like you, who also contacted us. Although there is ample precedent for commercial use of spiritually theme music, we have decided to change to a passage from Wagner's *Tannhäuser* Overture, which music experts have assured us does not have religious importance. The new music will begin airing in June.'

I think that says it all! I find it absolutely abominable. Now we have the whole association for descriptive marketing in the United States, which is how to use music as description and how to market it that way, what they are saying to the public is you don't have to concentrate, you don't have to listen, you don't have to know anything about it, just come and you will find some association, and we will show you so many things that have nothing to do with the music and this way you will go into the music. Is that the answer to the so-called crisis in classical music?

Accessibility does not come through populism, accessibility comes through more interest and more knowledge, and not telling people don't worry you'll be all right, just sit there, buy your ticket, sit there, shut your ears, and you will think of something. That is what we are telling them. This is criminal, and this is something which has bothered me more and more and more over the years. Music in itself has nothing to do with a society that in a way rejects what I would call publicly accepted standards of life, and of intelligence, and of human existence, and takes the easy way out with a kind of political correctness which does only a few things, all of them, in my view, negative.

It shows you how to hide your real feelings, it shows you how to cope with the fact that you are not allowed to show dislike of anything, and I wonder how long it takes before the not showing of dislike also goes on to the showing of like. The society that has accepted so many rules, so many regulations, and so many procedures, has the great advantage of avoiding situations of conflict. This is very positive, very useful, and very necessary; however when taken beyond the human level it brings us to the point where there is no more conflict, but there is also no more contact.

This is in a way what I wanted to share with you, that music teaches us exactly this. Conflict, difference of opinion, is the very essence of music, in the balance, in the dynamic, in the way that the music is written. You see that in a Bach fugue, you see that in Mozart concertos and operas, the subversiveness sometimes of the accompaniment. Music teaches us that it is precisely our capacity to bring all the different elements together in a sense of proportion so that they lead to a sense of a whole, and this is what I feel, in my own subjective way, is one of the main lessons that I have learned from music for life.

Having started very young I was put in contact very early on with the question, how does a child of twelve or fourteen without life experience, how can he express the mature thoughts of a Beethoven? And of course he can't. There's a lot of things that I have learned from my experiences in life since then that I feel I try every day to put into the music, but there is a lot more. A lot more that I have learned from observing music: not as a specialised phenomenon of sound, not only as a specialisation or profession, but as something which can teach us many things about ourselves and about life.

2005

Alec Broers

The Triumph of Technology

Extract from 'Technology will Determine the
Future of the Human Race'

Baron Alec Broers (born 1938), is a British electrical engineer, born in India and educated in Australia and England, who is the former president of the Royal Academy of Engineering. His Reith Lecture series examined how technology can and should hold the key to the future of the human race. In this first lecture, Broers argues that man's way of life has depended on technology since the beginning of civilisation, but questions whether society is coping with the newest cascade of technological advances.

Four thousand years ago, just five miles north of present day Thetford, our Neolithic ancestors began what may have been the largest early industrial process in these islands. This is the site that the Anglo-Saxons called 'Grimes Graves' and it contains nearly four hundred mineshafts, built to extract high-quality flints, which could be chipped to produce sharp cutting edges. Using nothing but tools of bone and wood, and presumably the flints themselves, these ancient people excavated to a depth of up to twelve metres, to reach the buried flints. It has been calculated that the miners needed to remove a thousand tonnes of waste to produce eight tonnes of flint. The site covers nearly forty hectares and the whole project is astonishing.

Whilst more advanced technologies had developed else-where – for instance in China – our ancestors' task was anything but easy. They needed timbers to shore up their excavations and ladders to get down in to them; lighting was required in the deeper pits; and they needed tools, which they made from deer antlers, so they had to manage the local herds of red deer. A separate and skilled industry was required to work the extracted flints and to market and distribute them. The flints were used as axe heads, as agricultural implements, as arrow-heads, and no doubt there were countless other applications that we have lost track of. The Grimes Graves operation underpinned the foundations of a new sort of society. The timescale was quite different from our own. Excavation at Grimes Graves lasted more than five centuries, whereas, for example, valve electronics lasted about fifty years.

Humankind's way of life has depended on technology since the beginning of civilisation. It can indeed be argued that civilisation began when humans first used technologies, moving away from the merely instinctual and into an era when people began to impose themselves on their environment, going beyond mere existence, to a way of life which enabled them to take increasing advantage of their intellect. A visit to Grimes Graves at its peak would have created as much wonder as was created by flight or the telephone when they first appeared.

Ranking in importance such early developments as the techniques of flint extraction against subsequent developments, such as the use of metals, is not easy, especially as the primitive technologies were independently developed in widely separated societies. But any such ranking is fraught with difficulties. A recent poll asked the public how they would rank Britain's greatest inventions: electricity generation, which is the foundation of almost every current technology; the jet engine, which made possible our international mobility; the invention of vaccination that saved millions of lives; the discovery of the structure of DNA, which underpins biotechnology; the possibilities seemed endless. Well, the public chose none of these, but instead . . . the safety bicycle. And it was that choice which confirmed my subject for these lectures.

The bicycle is of course an ingenious, practical and sustainable invention, which brought new opportunities for people in every stratum of society, and which continues to offer benefits today. But to place it ahead of the fundamental accomplishments of Faraday, Stephenson, Maxwell, Thomson, Whittle, and Crick & Watson demonstrates in my mind a profound misunderstanding of the contribution of advanced technologies to our lives, and of the vast pyramid of scientific and technical achievement that underlies these technologies.

The means to control plagues, to travel in hours to parts of the world which once took months to reach, to be able to access billions of written words from one's desk, to instantly conjure up high-quality images of distant objects and events – these are just a few of the technologies which we take almost for granted and which rest upon the accomplishments of generations of British engineers and scientists. Compared with these, I am afraid I cannot view the safety bicycle as a significant contender. But the fact that so many of our compatriots thought that it was of such paramount significance surely indicates a failure – of serious dimensions – in communication and understanding.

My contention is that technology is sidelined and undervalued – we become defensive about it and would rather retreat into the past, or into fundamental science, than to strive to stay in the race. The cost of this major social failure will progressively disadvantage all of us. Technology is determining the future of the human race. We need it to satisfy our appetite for energy, perhaps through nuclear power; to help us address hunger through plant breeding throughout the world; to monitor and find the means for avoiding global warming so that we can rescue our planet for future generations. Technology can improve our health, and lengthen our lives. Technology, I repeat, will determine the future of the human race. We should recognise this and give it the profile and status that it deserves.

The most straightforward explanation for the lack of appreciation is that modern technologies are too complex to be understood by anyone but the experts. But this is only true if the details are to be understood. It is up to the engineers and scientists who create these technologies to explain what they have done in language that can be understood by non-experts. We are very much to blame.

Mind you, matters were no better in days gone by when those responsible for the developments were purposefully obscure about their discoveries. The boundary between science and what for the sake of simplicity we call 'magic' was blurred. Even when the Royal Society, Great Britain's leading scientific academy, was founded in 1662 its objectives included matters we would now class as 'alchemy' rather than science. Knowledge was power and potentates were anxious to restrain its diffusion. Galileo was condemned and confined to house arrest for the latter part of his life for seeking to promulgate theories we now know to have been broadly correct. Worse perhaps than that, he wrote in the vernacular language (Italian) which could be understood by ordinary people, rather than the Latin of the scholars. Even the humdrum mining at Grimes Graves seems to have been associated with mystical rituals and ceremonies. The demystification of science is another change of the last few centuries, but it is evidently one which remains incomplete.

One of the reasons that the earliest significant advances were few and far between was that the technologies of communication had yet to be created, and communication of any kind could be rigidly controlled. While there was only word of mouth, information must frequently have been lost, and the process of innovation forced to repeat itself over and over again. Innovation could not advance exponentially as it does today because there were no means reliably to pass information from generation to generation, or between widely separated societies. The difficulty of transportation compounded the problem: it was only the wealthy and powerful who could travel to distant sources of information. It was through primitive paintings and tablets of stone, and eventually handwritten manuscripts, that each generation first began to preserve and reliably to pass on its precious knowledge.

Progress remained slow because it was only through tedious hand-copying that more than a single record could be produced, and replication in large numbers was impossible. It was the printing press that began to solve this problem. Printing was the first and perhaps the greatest of the communication technologies. It was followed four centuries later by the telegraph and then the telephone, the radio, the television and now, and perhaps as important in its influence as the early printing presses, the electronic media, especially the internet. Electronic networks provide the ability to communicate instantaneously anywhere in the world and the World Wide Web of Tim Berners-Lee makes – in principle – all of the information possessed by anyone available to everyone.

This previously inconceivable connectivity enables people to contribute to the process of innovation, or perhaps more importantly, to avoid the mistakes of others. Yet every advance in communication technology has facilitated the dissemination of both misinformation and disinformation; the more advanced the technology the greater the potential for misuse. The internet is especially vulnerable as it is less controlled than its predecessors, and the World Wide Web Consortium is fighting to keep it this way for reasons I support, but the inevitable consequence is that it carries a plethora of falsehood, which any surf of the web will speedily demonstrate. We must arm ourselves against such falsehood – teach people to be intelligent critics and help them judge whether a source is reliable.

The ready availability of even objective truth doesn't mean that objective truth will be believed or absorbed. For example, the difficulty the public has in understanding science in some respects grows rather than shrinks in the age of unlimited information. The Royal Institution of London was specifically founded – mainly by non-scientists – to 'diffuse the knowledge, and to facilitate the general introduction, of useful mechanical inventions and improvements, and to teach the application of science to the common purposes of life'. Those rotund eighteenth-century phrases contain a mighty truth which we need to heed no less today.

Advances in technology accelerated as efforts to understand the world around us bore fruit. For instance, inherited folk lore in medicine began to crumble in the light of advances in understanding made by William Harvey and others, based on systematic observation and recording. Newton put to flight so many of the myths about the universe. Newton's 'laws' introduced systematic and (on the face of things) simple rules which helped to explain the Universe, and helped to solve previously insoluble problems. This was the beginning of a new era. Perversely, it was also when intellectual advances began to become so complex that it became difficult and eventually impossible for the non-specialist to understand them.

Technologies have grown more complex, and yet – despite hugely expanded public education – understanding of them has diminished. The idea of a straight-line development towards an ideal is attractive, but it is alas untrue. There have been mistakes in judgement, mistakes sometimes compounded by secrecy. In health-related issues there is the tragedy of Thalidomide, to mention one example. Engineers, whilst making immense leaps in so many directions, have failed always to predict other consequences of operating in hitherto unknown regimes: the amazingly innovative British jet airliner, the Comet, ahead of all its competitors at the time, was aborted because of insufficient understanding of materials and stress-induced fatigue. Such lapses have tended to engender a sense of mistrust and suspicion on the part of the general public, and there is an ever-more pressing need for scientists and engineers openly to communicate what they are doing and to be candid over the likely consequences of their work.

I have found that the possession of an understanding of technology, just as with an understanding of music, literature, or the arts, brings with it great personal satisfaction and pleasure. I still pause to wonder at the achievements of humankind, for example, when I am flying in comfort at 40,000 feet and look down on the white caps and spume of a turbulent sea so far distant below me, and realise the difficulties there were in crossing it only a couple of lifetimes ago. I know that I can safely drink the water that runs out of the tap in the majority of places I visit in the world, and can talk with my family or even hold in my hand a real-time picture of them wherever I am. How remarkable it is to gaze up at the moon and the planets and realise that we have already walked on that great sphere and have sent intelligent machines to those planets, even to their satellites, and received high-quality pictures and data from those remote surfaces.

My appreciation is all the greater because I know enough to realise how difficult it has been to accomplish these things, enough in fact to know how little – after a lifetime in engineering and science – I actually know myself. I sometimes play the game of wondering how much I would be able to recreate if by some cataclysmic disaster I were to be the only person left with knowledge of how these wonders were accomplished. I am afraid that it would only be a small and specialised fraction of electronics.

I was born in Calcutta. My father was an insurance businessman, but his great passion was for technology, especially wireless and photography. Indeed, he spent enough time on these hobbies that his expertise was close to professional. His interest in radio is recorded in a series of articles that he wrote for the Calcutta Statesman in the late 1930s discussing radio and reviewing the latest receivers. He was one of the first to receive the BBC on short-wave radio and he wrote under the pseudonym 'Superhet'. Radios and TVs still use superheterodyne receivers but that will have to be the subject of another series of lectures. By happy coincidence, but perhaps not surprisingly, he wrote twice about Sir John Reith, describing him in 1938, the year I was born, as, 'building up the BBC from its beginnings to the mighty machine which today transmits music, entertainment and information to no less than 8,600,000 homes in Great Britain'.

That so many people are able to hear this lecture is itself the consequence of a whole series of inventions and coincidences. Whilst some of the basic principles of radio were understood, the fundamental roots of broadcasting arrived partly by chance, as a technology thought of as the opportunity for 'messages without wires' turned unintentionally into a system of diffusion to multiple audiences. The development of the valve, 'the magic lamp of radio', was the decisive step, but so were the governmental and regulatory attitudes that followed and which for a time seemed likely to snuff out infant broadcasting.

No one could anticipate the effects of the radio, on the printed word, on politics, on social behaviour, on advertising, even following that fateful day in 1922 when the first radio commercial was broadcast. The future US President, Herbert Hoover, said of this afterwards that it was 'inconceivable that we should allow so great a possibility for service . . . to be drowned out by advertising chatter'. We all know what happened to that good intention, but at least the BBC and National Public Radio in the USA hold out against that chatter.

There was, you can be sure, no lack of commentators eager to predict the worst outcomes of radio broadcasting, that it would destroy theatres and newspapers, that it would vulgarise culture, things which turned out either to be untrue or which were outweighed by the benefits. Through radio and later television, and subsequently the internet, societies beyond the metropolitan circle – and beyond the 'rich' world – have access to music, literature, drama, information and news, in a way that was previously impossible.

Perhaps because we have yet to come fully to terms with their implications and possibilities, the potentialities of modern technology tend to be thought of in terms of advances brought about by computers and electronic communications, and indeed those potentialities are awesome. But is it not developments in transport, medicine, energy and weaponry that have produced the greatest impact upon our lives?

It is surely by developments in medicine that the greatest numbers of the world's peoples have been most immediately affected. Changed techniques for travel have had revolutionary social consequences, at least in the first world. Some of the technologies of energy generation are threatening the planet's eco-system (and their profligate use of scarce non-renewable resources presents still greater threats in the future). Finally, we are unlikely to overlook the implications of weaponry and its delivery. These have shifted centres of power and have had unpredictable and as yet unforeseen effects on the relative success of different countries and societies. The twentieth century, the seed-bed of so many advanced sciences, was also the century of previously unimaginable atrocities based on advances in technology and the capacity for yet-greater atrocities clearly still exists.

I would argue, though, that most new technologies, with the exception of those associated with weaponry, have had hugely beneficial effects for most people, extending our capabilities and indeed our lives to an extent that our ancestors could not have imagined and I believe that we are only at the beginning.

We began in the empty landscape of East Anglia, four millennia ago. The basis of the highest achievement in their day, flints were superseded as a fundamental technology by metals of increasing sophistication. Now they are but historic artefacts. Other, far more complex, technologies have followed a similar course, passing from the mainstream into recreation, heritage, and history. One thinks of the sailing ship and the steam locomotive, although Ellen MacArthur's heroic sailing triumphs suggest that technology developments in sailing are still alive and well

The cycle of technological change grows faster. Compared with the sailing ship, how brief was the longevity of the steam engine, let alone the vinyl gramophone record? What will be the next cycle, and how will it emerge? I hope it is clear by now that I am convinced that it is technology that shapes our lives and that its influence is paramount and is only going to increase as time passes. It is time that we in Britain, so good at fundamental science, also came fully to appreciate the intellectual challenge behind product development. We seem culturally unable to realise that this can be more challenging than fundamental science and requires the very best minds. This has already been grasped in India and China which in my view is pleasing because, after all, technology is the means by which the developing world can increase its standard of living. But if we do not join the race to advance technology we face serious consequences, not least that we will fall behind in our own intellectual, social and material development.

V. S. Ramachandran

The Emerging Mind

Extract from 'Phantoms in the Brain'

Professor Vilayanur S. Ramachandran (born 1951), is an Indian neuroscientist. His Reith Lecture series explored new insights into the human brain's workings. In this excerpt from his first lecture, Ramachandran argues that scientists need no longer be afraid to ask the big questions about what it means to be human, and how by studying neurological syndromes we can acquire novel insights into the functions of the normal brain.

The history of mankind in the last three hundred years has been punctuated by major upheavals in human thought that we call scientific revolutions – upheavals that have profoundly affected the way in which we view ourselves and our place in the cosmos. But now, we are poised for the greatest revolution of all – understanding the human brain. This will surely be a turning point in the history of the human species for, unlike those earlier revolutions in science, this one is not about the outside world, not about cosmology or biology or physics, but about ourselves, about the very organ that made those earlier revolutions possible. And I want to emphasise that these insights into the human brain will have a profound impact not just on us scientists but also on the humanities, and indeed they may even help us bridge what C. P. Snow called the two cultures – science on the one hand and arts, philosophy and humanities on the other.

Given the enormous amount of research on the brain, all I can do is to provide a very impressionistic survey rather than try to be comprehensive. Of course by doing this, I will be oversimplifying many of the issues involved and run the risk of annoying some of my specialist colleagues. But, as Lord

Reith himself once said, 'There are some people whom it is one's duty to offend!'

The human brain, it has been said, is the most complexly organised structure in the universe and to appreciate this you just have to look at some numbers. The brain is made up of one hundred billion nerve cells, or 'neurons', which are the basic structural and functional units of the nervous system. Each neuron makes something like a thousand to ten thousand contacts with other neurons and these points of contact are called synapses, where exchange of information occurs. And based on this information, someone has calculated that the number of possible permutations and combinations of brain activity, in other words the numbers of brain states, exceeds the number of elementary particles in the known universe.

Even though it's common knowledge these days, it never ceases to amaze me that all the richness of our mental life – all our feelings, our emotions, our thoughts, our ambitions, our love life, our religious sentiments and even what each of us regards us as his own intimate private self – is simply the activity of these little specks of jelly in your head, in your brain. There is nothing else.

Given the staggering complexity, where do you even begin? Well let's start with some basic anatomy. It's the twenty-first century and most people here have a rough idea what the brain looks like. It's got two mirror-image halves, called the cerebral hemispheres, so it looks like a walnut sitting on top of a stalk, called the brain stem, and each hemisphere is divided into four lobes, the frontal lobe, the parietal lobe, the occipital lobe and the temporal lobe. The occipital lobe in the back is concerned with vision. If it's damaged, you become blind. The temporal lobe is concerned with things like hearing, with emotions and certain aspects of perception. The parietal lobes of the brain – at the sides of the head – are concerned with creating a three-dimensional representation of the spatial layout of the external world, and also of your own body in that three-dimensional representation. And lastly the frontal lobes, in the front, are the most mysterious of all. They are concerned with some very enigmatic aspects of human mind and human behaviour such as your moral sense, your wisdom, your ambition and other activities of the mind which we know very little about.

There are several ways of studying the brain but my approach is to look at people who have had some sort of damage to a small part of the brain, or some change in a small part of the brain. Interestingly, when you look at these people who have had a small lesion in a specific part of the brain, what you see is not an across-the-board reduction in all their cognitive capacities or a blunting of their mind; what you see is often a highly selective loss of one specific function with other functions being preserved intact, and this gives you some confidence in asserting that that part of the brain is somehow involved in mediating that function. To give you a flavour for this kind of research, I'm going to mention some of my favourite examples.

With a phantom limb, a patient has an arm amputated but the patient continues to vividly feel the presence of that arm, because their brain gets cross-wired. However, a similar sort of cross-wiring can happen because of a mutation, if there is something wrong with your genes. Instead of the brain modules remaining segregated, you get this accidental cross-wiring and then you get a curious condition called synaesthesia, which we have now been studying. Briefly, it was described by Francis Galton in the nineteenth century: he pointed out that some people who are perfectly normal in other respects have one peculiar symptom, if you want to call it a symptom. These people, who are otherwise completely normal, get their senses mixed up so every time they hear a particular tone they see a particular colour. C sharp is red, F sharp is blue, another tone might be indigo. This phenomenon, this mingling of senses, is synaesthesia. Galton pointed out that it runs in families; we and others have confirmed this, including Simon Baron-Cohen.

Another aspect of this syndrome is that whenever you hear a particular tone you see a particular colour. Some of these people also find that when they see numbers in black and white, like the number 5 or the number 6 or the number 7, what we call Arabic numerals – Indian numerals strictly speaking – it evokes a particular colour. So 5 is always red, 6 is always green, 7 is always indigo, 8 is always yellow. This again is another example of synaesthesia and it's very common. We find it's about one in two hundred people who have this, so it's not as rare as people have thought it to be in the past.

Why does this happen? Why does this mixing of signals occur? A student of mine, Ed Hubbard, and I were looking at brain maps, and we were struck by the fact that if you look at the fusiform gyrus – that's where the colour information is analysed. But, amazingly, the number area of the brain, which represents visual graphemes of numbers, is right next to it, also in the fusiform gyrus, almost touching it. So we said this can't be a coincidence. Maybe in some people there is some accidental cross-wiring, just as after amputation we get cross-wiring between the face and the hand, in these people maybe there's a cross-wiring between the number and colour area in the fusiform gyrus. Of course the key difference in the case of phantom limbs is that it's the amputation which causes the reorganisation, whereas in synaesthesia – given that it runs in families – we think it's caused by a gene or a set of genes which causes abnormal connections between adjacent brain regions, in this case between numbers and colours.

Even though the phenomenon was described by Galton a hundred years ago, it's been regarded mainly as a curiosity. Many neuroscientists in the past thought these people were just crazy or faking it to draw attention to themselves. Or maybe it's childhood memories – you played with refrigerator magnets and 5 was red, 6 was blue, 7 was green. This argument never made much sense to me because why does it then run in families? You'd have to say maybe the same magnets were passed round.

So the first thing we wanted to show was that this is a real phenomenon, it's the person genuinely seeing red when he sees 5; it's not just imagination or memory. How do you show that? We devised a simple display on the computer screen, a number of 5s scattered on the screen, just black and white. Embedded among those 5s are a number of 2s and these 2s form a hidden shape, like a triangle or a square. Now when any one of us 'normals' or less-gifted individuals, looks at this pattern, you see nothing. But when a synaesthete who sees numbers as colour looks at it, he sees the 5s as red and the 2s as green so instantly the 2s pop out and he says 'oh, they're forming a triangle!'; they are much better at doing this than normal people, so it's a clinical test for discovering synaesthetes.

Now, the fact that synaesthetes are actually better at this than normal people suggests that they can't be crazy. If they're crazy, how come they're better at it? It shows this is a genuine sensory phenomenon. It also shows that it can't be memory association or something cognitive or a metaphor because – if that were true, how come he's able to see the triangle or the square pop out from the background? We have shown that this phenomenon is real; through experiments to test the idea there's actual cross-wiring in the brain and have shown that in fact there's activation of the fusiform gyrus in the colour area just showing numbers to these people.

But then the next question is: here are some people with

some quirk in the brain who see numbers as colours, so why should I care? Well I'm going to show you that you're all synaesthetes but you're in denial about it. What I want you to do is imagine two shapes in front of you. Imagine that one of them is a shattered piece of glass with jagged edges, while the other is like an amoeba, it's got undulating curvy shapes. And one of them I'm going to call a bouba, and the other is kiki. Which is which? The amazing thing is that 98 per cent of people will pick the shattered piece of glass with the jagged edges, and say 'oh that's a kiki', and the undulating amoeboid shape, 'oh that's a bouba', even though they have never seen the shape before. Why does this happen? Well, I suggest it happens because you're all synesthetes.

I'll briefly tell you about another syndrome that is even more bizarre, and this is pain asymbolia. I saw a patient in Vellore in India about ten years ago, who was quite intellectually normal, mentally quite lucid, alert, attentive, his memory was normal, perception, everything was fine. Except, when I took a needle and pricked him to determine the intactness of his pain pathways, he started giggling. He told me 'Doctor, I feel the pain but it doesn't hurt. It feels very funny, like a tickle', and he would start laughing uncontrollably.

Here is the ultimate irony – a human being laughing in the face of pain. Why would the patient do this? Well, seeing this patient made me ask an even more basic question: why does anybody laugh? It is a species-specific trait, laughter. A martian ethologist watching you all today would be very surprised because every now and then all of you here stop what you're doing, shake your head, make this funny staccato rhythmic sound, hyena-like sound. Why do you do it? Now clearly laughter is hard-wired, it's a 'universal' trait. You see it in every society, every civilisation, every culture, society, has some form of laughter and humour – except the Germans.

This suggests strongly that it's hard-wired in the brain and this raises an interesting question. Why did it evolve in the brain? How did it evolve through natural selection? When you look at all jokes and humour across societies, the common denominator of all jokes and humour despite all the diversity is that you take a person along a garden path of expectation and at the very end you suddenly introduce an unexpected twist that entails a complete reinterpretation of all the previous facts. That's called a punchline of the joke. Now obviously that is not sufficient for laughter because then every great scientific discovery or every 'paradigm shift' would be funny, and my scientific colleagues wouldn't find it amusing if I said their discoveries were funny.

The key ingredient here is it's not merely sufficient that you introduce a reinterpretation, but the reinterpretation, the new model you have come up with, should be inconsequential, it should be of trivial consequence. It sounds a bit abstract so let me illustrate with a concrete example. Here is a portly gentleman walking along, he is trying to reach his destination, but before he does that he slips on a banana peel and falls. And then he breaks his head and blood spills out and obviously you are not going to laugh. You are going to rush to the telephone and call the ambulance. But imagine instead of that, he walks along, slips on the banana peel, falls, wipes off the goo from his face, looks around him everywhere, and then gets up, then you start laughing. The reason is because now you know it's inconsequential, you say, 'Oh it's no big deal, there's no real danger here.' So what I'm arguing is, laughter is nature's false alarm. Why is this useful from an evolutionary standpoint? What you are doing with this rhythmic staccato sound of laughter is informing your kin who share your genes, don't waste your precious resources rushing to this person's aid, it's a false alarm, everything is OK. It's nature's OK signal.

What has this got to do with my patient in Vellore? Let me explain. When we examined his brain through a CT scan, we found there was damage to the region called the insular cortex on the sides of the brain. The insular cortex receives pain signals from the viscera and from the skin; that's where you experience the raw sensation of pain, but it turns out there are many layers to pain. It's not just a unitary thing. From the insular cortex the message goes to the amygdala, and then to the rest of the limbic system, and especially the anterior cingulate, where you respond emotionally to the pain, and take the appropriate action. So my idea was, maybe what's happened on this patient is, the insular cortex is normal – that's why he says, doctor I can feel the pain – but the message, the wire that goes from the insular to the rest of the limbic system and the anterior cingulate, is cut.

Therefore you have the two key ingredients you need for laughter and humour, namely one part of the brain signalling a potential danger, 'My god there is something painful here', but the very next instant the anterior cingulate says, 'But I'm not getting any signal; big deal, there is no danger here, forget it.' So you have the two key ingredients and the patient starts laughing and giggling uncontrollably.

I would like to conclude with a quotation from my previous book, *Phantoms in the Brain*:

> There is something distinctly odd about a hairless, neotenous primate that has evolved into a species that can look back over its own shoulder to ponder its own origins. Odder still, the brain cannot only discover how other brains work but also ask questions about itself. Who am I? What is the meaning of my existence, especially if you are from India? Why do I laugh? Why do I dream, why do I enjoy art, music and poetry? Does my mind consist entirely of the activity of neurons in my brain? If so, what scope is there for free will? It is the peculiar recursive quality of these questions as the brain struggles to understand itself that makes neurology so fascinating. The prospect of answering these questions in the next millennium is both exhilarating and disquieting, but it's surely the greatest adventure that our species has ever embarked upon.

HRH The Prince of Wales

—◠◡—

Respect for the Earth

Extract from 'A Royal View'

During the millennium year, five Reith lecturers (Chris Patten, Tim Lovejoy, Sir John Browne, Dr Gro Harlem Brundtland and Dr Vandana Shiva) discussed one of the most pressing issues of our time – sustainable development. HRH The Prince of Wales delivered his own speech as part of the series, urging listeners to 'reacknowledge a sense of the sacred in our dealings with the natural world'.

Like millions of other people around the world, I have been fascinated to hear five eminent speakers share with us their thoughts, hopes and fears about sustainable development, based on their own experience.

All five of those contributions have been immensely thoughtful and challenging. There have been clear differences – of opinion and of emphasis – between the speakers, but there have also been some important common themes – both implicit and explicit. One of those themes has been the suggestion that sustainable development is a matter of enlightened self-interest. Two of the speakers used this phrase, and I don't believe that the other three would dissent from it – and nor would I. Self-interest is a powerful motivating force for all of us, and if we can somehow convince ourselves that sustainable development is in all our interests then we will have taken a valuable first step towards achieving it.

But self-interest comes in many competing guises, not all of which – I fear – are likely to lead in the right direction for very long, nor to embrace the manifold needs of future generations. I am convinced we will need to dig rather deeper to find the inspiration, sense of urgency and moral purpose required to confront the hard choices which face us on the long road to sustainable development. So although it seems to have become deeply unfashionable to talk about the spiritual dimension of our existence, that is what I propose to do.

The idea that there is a sacred trust between mankind and our Creator, under which we accept a duty of stewardship for the Earth, has been an important feature of most religious and spiritual thought throughout the ages. Even those whose beliefs have not included the existence of a Creator have, nevertheless, adopted a similar position on moral and ethical grounds. It is only recently that this guiding principle has become smothered by almost impenetrable layers of scientific rationalism.

I believe that if we are to achieve genuinely sustainable development we will first have to rediscover, or reacknowledge, a sense of the sacred in our dealings with the natural world, and with each other. If literally nothing is held sacred any more – because it is considered synonymous with superstition, or in some other way 'irrational' – what is there to prevent us treating our entire world as some 'great laboratory of life', with potentially disastrous long-term consequences?

Fundamentally, an understanding of the sacred helps us to acknowledge that there are bounds of balance, order and harmony in the natural world which set limits to our ambitions and define the parameters of sustainable development.

In some cases, Nature's limits are well understood at the rational, scientific level. As a simple example, we know that trying to graze too many sheep on a hillside will, sooner or later, be counter-productive, for the sheep, the hillside, or both. More widely, we understand that the over-use of insecticides or antibiotics leads to problems of resistance. And we are beginning to comprehend the full, awful consequences of pumping too much carbon dioxide into the earth's atmosphere. Yet the actions being taken to halt the damage known to be caused by exceeding Nature's limits in these and other ways are insufficient to ensure a sustainable outcome.

In other areas, such as the artificial and uncontained transfer of genes between species of plants and animals, the lack of hard scientific evidence of harmful consequences is regarded, in many quarters, as sufficient reason to allow such developments to proceed. The idea of taking a precautionary approach, in this and many other potentially damaging situations, receives overwhelming public support, but still faces a degree of official opposition, as if admitting the possibility of doubt was a sign of weakness or even of a wish to halt 'progress'. On the contrary, I believe it to be a sign of strength and of wisdom.

It seems that when we do have scientific evidence that we are damaging our environment we aren't doing enough to put things right, and when we don't have that evidence we are prone to do nothing at all, regardless of the risks. Part of the problem is the prevailing approach that seeks to reduce the natural world, including ourselves, to the level of nothing more than a mechanical process. For whilst the natural theologians of the eighteenth and nineteenth centuries, like

Thomas Morgan, referred to 'the perfect unity, order, wisdom and design' of the natural world, scientists, like Bertrand Russell, rejected this idea as rubbish. 'I think the Universe', he wrote, 'is all spots and jumps without unity and without continuity, without coherence or orderliness'. Sir Julian Huxley wrote in *Evolution: the modern synthesis* that 'modern science must rule out special creation or divine guidance'.

But why? As Professor Alan Linton of Bristol University has written – 'evolution is a man-made "theory" to explain the origin and continuance of life on this planet without reference to a Creator'. It is because of our inability or refusal to accept the existence of a guiding Hand that Nature has come to be regarded as a system that can be engineered for our own convenience, or as a nuisance to be evaded and manipulated, and in which anything that happens can be 'fixed' by technology and human ingenuity. Fritz Schumacher recognised the inherent dangers in this approach when he said that 'there are two sciences – the science of manipulation and the science of understanding'.

In this technology-driven age it is all too easy for us to forget that mankind is a part of Nature, and not apart from it, and that this is why we should seek to work with the grain of Nature in everything we do. For the natural world is, as the economist Herman Daly puts it, 'the envelope that contains, sustains and provisions the economy' – not the other way round. So which argument do you think will win – the living world as one, or the world made up of random parts, the product of mere chance, thereby providing the justification for any kind of development?

This, to my mind, lies at the heart of what we call sustainable development. We need, therefore, to rediscover a reverence for the natural world, irrespective of its usefulness to ourselves – to become more aware, in Philip Sherrard's words, of the 'relationship of interdependence, interpenetration and reciprocity between God, Man and Creation'. Above all, we should show greater respect for the genius of Nature's designs – rigorously tested and refined over millions of years. This means being careful to use science to understand how Nature works – not to change what Nature is, as we do when genetic manipulation seeks to transform the process of biological evolution into something altogether different. The idea that the different parts of the natural world are connected through an intricate system of checks and balances which we disturb at our peril is all too easily dismissed as no longer relevant. So, in an age when we are told that science has all the answers, what chance is there for working with the grain of Nature?

As an example of working with the grain of Nature, I happen to believe that if a fraction of the money currently being invested in developing genetically manipulated crops were applied to understanding and improving traditional systems of agriculture, which have stood the all-important test of time, the results would be remarkable. There is already plenty of evidence of just what can be achieved through applying more knowledge and fewer chemicals to diverse cropping systems. These are genuinely sustainable methods. And they are far removed from the approaches based on monoculture which lend themselves to large-scale commercial exploitation, and which Vandana Shiva condemned so persuasively and so convincingly in her lecture.

Our most eminent scientists accept that there is still a vast amount that we don't know about our world and the life forms that inhabit it. As Sir Martin Rees, the Astronomer Royal, points out, it is complexity that makes things hard to understand, not size. In a comment which only an astronomer could make, he describes a butterfly as a more daunting intellectual challenge than the cosmos! Others, like Rachel Carson, have eloquently reminded us that we don't know how to make a single blade of grass. And St Matthew, in his wisdom, emphasised that not even Solomon in all his glory was arrayed as the lilies of the field . . .

Faced with such unknowns it is hard not to feel a sense of humility, wonder and awe about our place in the natural order. And to feel this at all stems from that inner, heartfelt reason which, sometimes despite ourselves, is telling us that we are intimately bound up in the mysteries of life and that we don't have all the answers. Perhaps, even, that we don't have to have all the answers before knowing what we should do in certain circumstances. As Blaise Pascal wrote in the seventeenth century, 'It is the heart that experiences God, not the reason'.

So do you not feel that, buried deep within each and every

one of us, there is an instinctive, heartfelt awareness that provides – if we will allow it to – the most reliable guide as to whether or not our actions are really in the long-term interests of our planet and all the life it supports? This awareness, this wisdom of the heart, may be no more than a faint memory of a distant harmony, rustling like a breeze through the leaves, yet sufficient to remind us that the earth is unique and that we have a duty to care for it.

Wisdom, empathy and compassion have no place in the empirical world, yet traditional wisdoms would ask, 'without them are we truly human?'. And it would be a good question. It was Socrates who, when asked for his definition of wisdom, gave as his conclusion, 'knowing that you don't know'.

In suggesting that we will need to listen rather more to the common sense emanating from our hearts if we are to achieve sustainable development, I am not suggesting that information gained through scientific investigation is anything other than essential. Far from it. But I believe that we need to restore the balance between the heartfelt reason of instinctive wisdom and the rational insights of scientific analysis. Neither, I believe, is much use on its own. So it is only by employing both the intuitive and the rational halves of our own nature – our hearts and our minds – that we will live up to the sacred trust that has been placed in us by our Creator – or our 'Sustainer', as ancient wisdom referred to the Creator.

As Gro Harlem Brundtland has reminded us, sustainable development is not just about the natural world, but about people too. This applies whether we are looking at the vast numbers who lack sufficient food or access to clean water, but also those living in poverty and without work. While there is no doubt that globalisation has brought advantages, it brings dangers too. Without the humility and humanity expressed by Sir John Browne in his notion of the 'connected economy' – an economy which acknowledges the social and environmental context within which it operates – there is the risk that the poorest and the weakest will not only see very little benefit but, worse, they may find that their livelihoods and cultures have been lost.

So, if we are serious about sustainable development then we must also remember that the lessons of history are particularly relevant when we start to look further ahead. Of course, in an age when it often seems that nothing can properly be regarded as important unless it can be described as 'modern', it is highly dangerous to talk about the lessons of the past. And are those lessons ever taught or understood adequately, in an age when to pass on a body of acquired knowledge of this kind is often considered prejudicial to 'progress'?

Of course, our descendants will have scientific and technological expertise beyond our imagining, but will they have the insight or the self-control to use this wisely, having learnt both from our successes and our failures? They won't, I believe, unless there are increased efforts to develop an approach to education which balances the rational with the intuitive.

Without this, truly sustainable development is doomed. It will merely become a hollow-sounding mantra that is repeated ad nauseam in order to make us all feel better. Surely, therefore, we need to look towards the creation of greater balance in the way we educate people so that the practical and intuitive wisdom of the past can be blended with the appropriate technology and knowledge of the present to produce the type of practitioner who is acutely aware of both the visible and invisible worlds that inform the entire cosmos.

The future will need people who understand that sustainable development is not merely about a series of technical fixes, about redesigning humanity or re-engineering Nature in an extension of globalised industrialisation – but about a reconnection with Nature and a profound understanding of the concepts of care that underpin long-term stewardship. Only by rediscovering the essential unity and order of the living and spiritual world – as in the case of organic agriculture or integrated medicine or in the way we build – and by bridging the destructive chasm between cynical secularism and the timelessness of traditional religion, will we avoid the dis-integration of our overall environment.

Above all, I don't want to see the day when we are rounded upon by our grandchildren and asked accusingly why we didn't listen more carefully to the wisdom of our hearts as well as to the rational analysis of our heads; why we didn't pay more attention to the preservation of bio-diversity and traditional communities or think more clearly about our role as stewards of creation. Taking a cautious approach, or achieving balance in life, is never as much fun as the alternatives, but that is what sustainable development is all about.

Richard Rogers

Sustainable City

Extract from 'The Culture of Cities'

Lord Richard Rogers of Riverside (born 1933), is an award-winning British-Italian architect, known for his work on high-profile projects such as the Pompidou Centre, Millennium Dome, and European Court of Human Rights. His lecture series focuses on architecture's social role and the sustainable urban development of towns and cities through social and environmental responsibility. In his first lecture, Rogers explores the fundamental dichotomy of the city; that it has the potential to both civilise and brutalise.

In 1957, the first satellite was launched into space to take its place amongst the stars. This signalled the birth of a new global consciousness, a dramatic change in our relationship to our planet. It gave us a place from which we could look at ourselves. From space, the beauty and fragility of the earth's atmosphere, our primordial support system are striking; but so, too, is humanity's systematic plundering of every aspect of our ecosystem. From space, we can see the scars of pollution, deforestation, industry and urban sprawl. Above us, the 400 or so satellites currently in orbit witness and gauge the global impact of a human population that has leapt from 1.5 to 5.5 billion in this century alone. Coldly they confirm the grim realities we all experience in our daily lives as we step out into the city.

It is a shocking revelation – especially to me as an architect – that the world's environmental crisis is being driven by our cities. For the first time in history, half the world's population live in cities. In 1900 it was only one-tenth. In thirty years, it may be as much as three-quarters. The urban population of the world is increasing at a rate of a quarter of a million people per day – think of it as a new London every month.

The scale, and the rate of increase, of our consumption

of resources, and the pollution it inflicts, is catastrophic. Let me offer you three examples to make the point. First, we take only 10 per cent of our energy from directly renewable and non-polluting sources, such as sun, wind and water. Yet in a single year, we burn some one million years' worth of non-renewable fossil fuels – coal, oil, gas – and this is producing the bulk of our pollution. Secondly, the Intergovernmental Panel on Climate Change has warned that a global warming mainly produced by the burning of fossil fuels is likely to cause a rise in temperature of three degrees centigrade by the end of the next century. Such a temperature increase could melt the ice cap and raise sea levels, enough to seriously threaten that half of the world's population which lives beside seas and rivers. My third example concerns the food chain. The World Resource Institute in Washington estimates that over the past fifty years 10 per cent of the vegetation-bearing surface of the earth has suffered moderate to extreme damage. In Britain alone, over-intensive farming, especially the overuse of fertilisers, has put more than a third of our soil at risk.

Human life has always depended on the three variables of population, resources and environment. But today, we are perhaps the first generation to face the simultaneous impact of expanding populations, depletion of resources and erosion of the environment. All this is common knowledge and yet, incredibly, industrial expansion carries on regardless.

Other societies have faced extinction; some, like the Easter Islanders of the Pacific, the Harappa civilisation of the Indus

Valley and the Teotihuacan of pre-Columbian America, due to ecological disasters of their own making. Historically societies unable to solve their environmental crisis have either migrated or become extinct. The vital difference today is that the scale of our crisis is no longer regional, but global: it involves all of humanity and the entire planet.

I believe that the same key trends that drive environmental decline are generating disastrous social instability. Social and environmental issues are interlocked, and cities, which are now failing to provide the most basic of needs of society, can provide a healthy and civilising environment for our citizens. I passionately believe that the art of city building has never been so crucial to our future.

My cause for optimism in the face of grim evidence comes from the growing acceptance of ecological thought. Scientists, philosophers, economists, architects and artists, often working with local communities, are now using a global perspective to explore strategies to sustain our future.

The United Nations report 'Our Common Future', laid down the concept of sustainable development as the backbone of a global economic policy; its aim that we should meet our present needs without compromising future generations, and that we should positively direct our development in favour of the world's majority: the poor. At the core of this concept is a new notion of wealth. This incorporates those environmental elements previously considered limitless and free – clean air, fresh water, an effective ozone layer, and a fertile land and sea.

The means proposed to protect the environment were stringent regulations and a costing of the market's use of natural resources: regulations – you don't use CFCs; costs – you pay for the damage your use of resources create. For example, by placing a tax on the use of coal or petrol, we both reflect the damage from acid rain and carbon dioxide and encourage the switch to renewable energies. The ultimate aim of sustainable economic development is to leave to future generations a stock of environmental wealth or national capital that equals or exceeds our own inheritance.

Nowhere is this sort of implementation of sustainability more relevant than in the city. In fact, I believe environmental 'sustainability' needs to become the guiding law of modern urban design – an innovation that would have an impact on the twenty-first-century city as radical as that of the industrial revolution on its nineteenth-century counterpart.

As it stands, cities and buildings are the most important destroyers of the ecosystem. In London, for example, massive traffic congestion causes more air pollution today than there was before the Clean Air Act banned the burning of coal in 1956. Foul air is blamed for the fact that one in seven city children in Britain now suffer from asthma.

In the United States, pollution rising from the cities has reduced crop production by 5 to 10 per cent. In Japan, Tokyo alone dumps an estimated 20 million tonnes of waste every year. The city has already saturated its bay with waste, and is now running out of sites on land. But although cities are breeding environmental disaster, there is nothing in the nature of city living that makes this inevitable. On the contrary, I believe that cities can be transformed into the most environmentally balanced form of modern settlement. Cities, and city living, can be designed to be more efficient and environmentally sustainable.

I have been focusing on the need for environmental reform, but I also want to stress that social aspects of city life are vital to a city's sustainability. We have to define sustainability in social and cultural terms, as well as environmental and economic ones. Poverty, unemployment, ill health, poor education – in short social injustice – all undermine a city's capacity to carry out these policies. An urban society in conflict, as in Grozny, or suffering severe poverty, as in Mexico City, or with large sections of the community alienated from mainstream life, as in Los Angeles, is unlikely to be persuaded about the importance of preserving natural resources, of switching to public transport. It is only if our cities offer a vibrant, healthy and secure urban life that we can dissuade people from fleeing to the suburbs.

Cities have grown and changed so much that it is hard to remember that they exist first and foremost for people. They are the cradle of civilisation, a place for societies to come together and exchange ideas. Cities concentrate physical, intellectual and creative energy. It is this social and cultural dynamic rather than an aesthetic balance created by the design of buildings that to my mind is the essence of civic beauty. I am passionate about the choice and diversity of city life – from exhibitions to demonstrations, from bars to cathedrals, and from shops to opera. I love the combination of ages, races, cultures and activities, the mix of community with anonymity, familiarity and surprise – even the sense of dangerous excitement they can generate. I enjoy the animation that pavement cafés bring to the street, the informal liveliness of the public square, the mixture of shops, offices and homes, that makes a living neighbourhood. Strolling through Europe's great public spaces – the covered Galleria in Milan, the Ramblas in Barcelona, or the parks of London, I feel part of the community of that city. The Italians even have a special word to describe the way men, women and children come out in the evening and stroll in the squares and streets, to see and be seen. They call it La Passeggiata.

One of the exhilarating moments of my career was when the Parisian authorities agreed to give half the site they had set aside for the Pompidou Centre to a public piazza. In the back of our minds, when we were planning how the centre could invigorate its surrounding streets and communities, was the bustling public square at the heart of Siena, scene of the great Palio horse race which thunders over its cobbles twice a year. Today, to my great delight, the Place Beaubourg and the Pompidou Centre teem with life, and this has led to a wholesale renewal of the area around it. I have been talking about the importance of a vibrant urban life – to my mind, the essential ingredient of a good city. And yet today this quality is increasingly missing. The public life of a city is enacted in its streets, squares, alleys and parks, and it is these spaces that make up the public domain.

This domain is an institution in its own right. It belongs to the community and, like any institution, it can enhance or frustrate our existence. But just ask anybody what they think of city life today. He or she will be more likely talk about congestion, pollution and fear of crime, than community, animation, or beauty. In all probability, a negative association will be made between city and quality of living.

The essential problem is that cities have been viewed in instrumental or consumerist terms. Those responsible for them have tended to see it as their role to design cities to meet private material needs, rather than to foster public life. The result is that cities have been polarised into communities of rich and poor and segregated into ghettoes of single-minded activity: the business park, the housing estate, the residential suburb – or, worse still – into giant, single-function buildings like shopping centres with their own private streets, which lead nowhere, built in.

The central distinction here is between what American political theorist Michael Walzer has called 'single-minded' and 'open-minded' spaces. The first is designed by planners and developers with only one purpose in view. The second caters for a variety of uses in which everyone can participate. The residential suburb, the housing estate, the business district and industrial zone, the car park, underpass, ring road, supermarket and shopping mall are all 'single-minded spaces'. The car is more single-minded than the train; the cinema is more single-minded than the museum; the fast-food restaurant is more single-minded than the pub. But the busy square, the lively street, the market, the park, the pavement café, are 'open-minded'. In the first set of spaces, we are generally in a hurry; but in 'open-minded' places, we are readier to meet people's gaze, to talk and to be waylaid.

Both types of space have a role to play in the city. Single-minded spaces cater to our very modern craving for private consumption, for autonomy and intimacy. They are, admittedly, very efficient. By contrast, 'open-minded places' give us something in common: they bring diverse sections of society together, and breed a sense of tolerance, identity and mutual respect.

My point, however, is that we have seen the first eclipsing the second. 'Openmindedness' has given way to 'single-mindedness'. We are witnessing the destruction of the very idea of the city. The emphasis is now on selfishness and separation rather than on contact and community. Businesses have been isolated and turned into commercial centres or business parks; shops into shopping centres, homes into residential suburbs and housing estates. The inevitable outcome is that streets, squares and other components of the public domain lose the very diversity that creates their animation. They become little more than functional spaces, highways for scurrying pedestrians or sealed private cars. I find it hard to believe that anyone would really be happy living in a city devoid of public life. Today's men and women may place a special value on privacy, but they also long for public life. The popularity of football matches and concerts, the dramatic increase of people going to museums, the crowds that pack Soho on a Friday and Saturday night all testify to this. If anything, we face the challenge of creating for the first time in history a truly inclusive, democratic public domain.

The absence of vibrant public spaces has dire social consequences. From Buenos Aires to Beijing, from Houston to Calcutta, we are launching cities on a spiral of decline. As cities become divided into ghettoes of activity, the spaces between them become increasingly soulless and cities themselves become less hospitable and more alienating. At some point in the spiralling descent, a new element enters: fear. As public spaces decline, we lose the natural policing of streets that comes from the very presence of people. Spaces in cities become territorial. Now they are perceived not merely as inhospitable but as positively dangerous. Gradually the semi-public spaces that once overlapped and enriched the public domain are privatised. The market becomes a shopping mall, the open university becomes a closed campus, and as this process spreads through the city, the public domain retreats. People who can afford it move out of the city or bar themselves in. Ultimately the city becomes a two-tier affair with the wealthy rushing from one protective enclave to another, and the poor trapped in inner city ghettos or – as in the growing cities of the developing world – in squalid shantytowns. We created cities to celebrate what we have in common. Now they are designed to keep us apart. It is in the sprawling cities of the United States – with their ghettos, heavily policed middle-class dormitories, shopping centres and business parks – that the tendencies I have identified can most clearly be seen.

In its time Los Angeles has inspired as much enthusiasm as any city on Earth. But the Californian writer Mike Davis has described how Los Angeles, the site of major riots, has grown more and more segregated and militarised. Starting at the outskirts, there is the Toxic Rim – a circle of giant garbage landfills, radioactive waste dumps and polluting industries. Moving inwards, you pass so-called 'gated' or privately patrolled residential suburbs and a zone of self-policing lower middle-class homes, until you reach a 'free-fire' downtown area of ghettos and gangs. Here, the Ramparts Division of Los Angeles Police regularly investigate more murders than any other local police department in the country. Finally, beyond this 'no-go area' lies the business district itself. In parts of this area, TV cameras and security devices screen almost every passing pedestrian. At the touch of a button, access is blocked, bulletproof screens are activated, bombproof shutters roll down. The appearance of the 'wrong sort of person' triggers a quiet panic: video cameras turn on their mounts, security guards adjust their belts. A new type of citadel has emerged, which relies not only on physical boundaries, high fences, barbed wire and imposing gates, but increasingly on invisible, electronic hardware.

And if Los Angeles has emerged as a modern fortress city, developments in Houston are almost as disturbing. An entire underground system, over six miles of passageway in all, has been dug beneath the city's downtown business area. This glitzy network, called with unintended irony 'the connection system', is entirely private. You cannot gain admittance from the street, but only from the marbled lobbies of banks and oil companies that dominate Houston. The result is the establishment of another form of urban ghetto. The car-dominated streets are left to the poor, mainly unemployed, while wealthy workers shop and do business in air-conditioned comfort and security. Of course our own cities are not yet like this, but many display the same characteristics writ small. We, too, have seen a retreat from the city and growing inner-city poverty, an increasing reliance on private security and private transport, the proliferation of one-dimensional spaces, and the explosion of riots. What I have been describing reflects the fundamental dichotomy of the city: its potential to civilise and its potential to brutalise.

But if we lament the recent transformation of our cities, we should acknowledge that cities can only reflect the values and character of the societies they contain. This relationship is well explored in the long tradition of attempts to make cities reflect society's ideals. Vitruvius, Leonardo da Vinci, Thomas Jefferson, Ebenezer Howard, Le Corbusier, Buckminster Fuller and others have proposed ideal urban forms to propel society through its traumas.

These architectural and social utopias exert a constant and profound influence on our great architects and patrons, and filter through to developers and city builders. In a democratic age, you might expect contemporary architecture to express democratic ideals and egalitarian values.

But recent transformations of cities reflect the workings of business committed to short-term profit, where the pursuit of wealth has become an end in itself, rather than a means to achieve broader goals. City planning world-wide is dominated by market forces, and short-term financial imperatives – an approach most spectacularly illustrated by the chaotic and office-dominated development on the Isle of Dogs in London. Not only have such developments eliminated variety of function from our city centres, but in this single-minded search for profit, we have ignored the needs of the wider community.

But if, as I have claimed, cities are where life is often at its most precarious, they are also where we have the greatest tangible opportunity for improvement, intervention and change.

I have been arguing that tenancies within our cities are working to undermine both the environment and their own social life. Putting cities back on the political agenda is now fundamental. What is needed is greater emphasis on citizens' participation in city design and planning. We must put communal objectives centre-stage. And should people doubt the possibility of regaining democratic control of their cities, examples from around the world prove them wrong. There are many countries where urbanism and architecture, in particular, are established public issues, and these provide a sharp contrast to recent British experience. In France, for example, President Mitterrand has stated that 'culture' – and first of all architecture – is the fourth highest voting issue. I dread to imagine where our politicians would rank culture.

Educating our children is a necessary first step towards involving communities in decision-making. It is on this that we must focus our National Curriculum. Teaching children about biology and history, but not about their actual environment – the built one – leaves them ill-equipped to participate in the process of respecting and improving the city that so critically affects their lives. We must teach citizenship and listen to citizens. So much of our future and our quality of life depends on getting this right.

Any type of close citizen involvement in city design requires us to make funds available to interest and inform the public. San Francisco has gone further and integrated the whole concept of public participation in urban planning into their electoral system. In local elections, you do not just choose a candidate, you have the opportunity to decide your own surroundings. How much office space should be allowed? Which dockside plan is the best?

Curitiba in Brazil has proved to be an object lesson for even the most deprived communities. Visionary leadership and open participation have transformed a once desolate shantytown into a thriving, self-reliant and expanding community with parks, public transport and good sanitation.

Finally, closer to home, Rotterdam is a good example of government-sponsored but community-led development. Here, much of the land is publicly-owned and can be given to the community when and where the need arises rather than when someone can afford to buy a site. The city grows in cell-like fashion, splitting and replicating into coherent neighbourhoods of between three to five thousand people, rather than sprawling and dividing into dormitory and work zones.

The approaches pursued in San Francisco, Curitiba or Rotterdam must not be taken as blueprints. In fact they illustrate how each city has evolved public administrations tailored to the culture and problems that its own communities face. What they do prove is that we can transform the fabric and environment of our cities through greater, genuine, public participation and committed government initiative. Throughout this lecture, I have emphasised the social problems and ecological crisis that contemporary cities and technologies are generating, but the answer to our problems lies not in turning our backs on technology but in embracing its pursuits and development.

Humankind's capacity to learn and to transmit accumulated knowledge from generation to generation, to anticipate and to solve problems is its greatest asset. I find it amazing that only seventy 70-year lifespans separate our own epoch, which has the ability to build a city in space, from the first mud cities along the Euphrates. It is the irrepressible power of the mind that has accelerated the development of our species. Knowledge, technology and our capacity for forethought has transformed our world, and often in the face of our own pessimism.

In 1798, the economist Malthus warned the world that the rate of population growth 'is infinitely greater than the power of the earth to feed future generations'. If he was proved wrong, as he was in the case of Britain, it was because he had not foreseen the remarkable capacity of technology. In the 100 years following his ominous prediction, the population of Britain quadrupled, but technological advances brought a fourteen-fold increase in agricultural production. The prospects that technology now offers are greater still. Only two 70-year lifespans separate the invention of the bicycle from the sinister perfection of the Stealth Bomber. Less than one lifespan separates the first electronic computer from the uncharted horizons of the information superhighway.

The problem is not with technology, but with its application. Today technology destabilises and transforms the modern age – as Marx famously said, 'All that is solid melts into air.' Caught in this endless upheaval, technology can be used to positive ends to advance social justice – one of modernity's greatest ideals. Perhaps we can say that when technology is used to secure the fundamentally modern principles of universal human rights – for shelter, food, health care, education and freedom – the modern age attains its full potential. It is here that the spirit of modernity finds its very expression.

The challenge we face today is to break with a system which treats technology and finance as a route to short-term profit rather than as a means to social and environmental ends. The urban planner who drives a motorway through the middle of a city merely to advance a single-minded goal of mobility employs technology for the wrong ends. So, too, do those developers and architects who design the largest, cheapest and most profitable building with no regard for a city's public life or environment. I am wild about science, not about science run wild. And that thought, I suppose, is at the heart of my concept of sustainability: the critical application of creative thinking and technology to secure our future on this small planet.

1990

Jonathan Sacks

The Persistence of Faith

Extract from 'The Environment of Faith'

Rabbi Lord Jonathan Sacks (born 1948), is a British religious leader, philosopher and author who served as Chief Rabbi of the United Hebrew Congregations of the Commonwealth for twenty-two years. In his Reith Lectures, he sought to examine the place of religion and ethics in a secular society. In this opening lecture, Sacks asks if modern cultures have forgotten their faith and reveals his reasons for believing that religion still offers the best moral framework for society.

There are moments when you can see the human landscape change before your eyes, and 1989 was one of them. In retrospect it will seem as significant a turning point in history as 1789, the year of the French Revolution and the birth of the secular state. Throughout Eastern Europe, communism appeared to crumble. The twentieth century had broken its greatest idols, the two versions of an absolute secular state: fascism, defeated in 1945, and communism last year. But what, in this revolution of the human spirit, lies ahead?

In the middle of it all, the American historian Francis Fukuyama wrote an article entitled 'The End of History'. In it he described the global spread of liberal democracy not as the triumph of an ideal, but as the victory of consumer culture. In the end, colour television had proved a more seductive prospect than the Communist Manifesto. Politics had moved beyond ideology. As Eduard Shevardnadze, the Soviet foreign minister, put it, 'the struggle between two opposing systems' had been superseded by the desire 'to build up material wealth at an accelerated rate'. Dialectical materialism was over; mail-order catalogue materialism had taken its place. Eastern Europe had discovered the discreet charm of the bourgeoisie.

It was, said Fukuyama, the end of history as we had known it: the struggle over ideas that had once called forth daring, courage and imagination. Instead, we would increasingly see societies based on nothing but the free play of choices and interests. What would absorb the human imagination would no longer be large and visionary goals but 'economic calculation, the endless solving of technical problems, environmental concerns, and the satisfaction of sophisticated consumer demands'. History would end not with the sound of apocalypse but the beat of a personal stereo.

Fukuyama's analysis takes us deep into irony. Because such a brave new world suggests a massive impoverishment of what we are as human beings, its accuracy as a prediction is matched only by its narrowness as a prescription. The human being as consumer neither is, nor can be, all we are, and a social system built on that premise will fail. The East has engaged in self-examination and has turned for inspiration to the West. But the West has yet to return the compliment and ask whether its own social fabric is in a state of good repair.

I believe it is not. And the problem lies not with our economic and political systems, but in a certain emptiness at the heart of our common life. Something has been lost in our consumer culture: that sense of meaning beyond ourselves that was expressed in our great religious traditions. It is not something whose eclipse we can contemplate with equanimity. Religious faith is central to a humane social order. To paraphrase a rabbinic saying: if we have only a secular society, even a secular society we will not have.

For some years, we have known that unrestricted pursuit of economic growth has devastated our physical environment. Pollution, waste and the depletion of natural resources have disturbed that 'narrow strip of soil, air and water . . . in which we live and move and have our being.' No one intended it. It happened. But, having happened, we can no longer ignore it, and whether our political commitments are blue or orange or red, we have all gone green. We have become aware that there are limits to growth.

But, as well as a physical ecology, we also inhabit a moral ecology: that network of beliefs, relationships and virtues within which we think, act and discover meaning. For the greater part of human history it has had a religious foundation. But for the past two centuries, in societies like Britain, that basis of belief has been profoundly eroded. And we know too much about ecological systems to suppose that you can remove one element and leave the rest unchanged. There is, if you like, a God-shaped hole in our ozone layer. And it's about time we thought about moral ecology too.

I speak from within the Jewish tradition, in which religion is more than what the individual does with his own solitude. God enters society in the form of specific ways of life, disclosed by revelation, mediated by tradition, embellished by custom and embodied in institutions. Faith lives not only in the privacy of the soul but in compassion and justice: the structures of our common life. The Hebrew Bible and the rabbis saw society as a covenant with God, and morality as a divine imperative. That tradition has deep echoes in Christianity and Islam as well, and has shaped our moral imagination.

To it we owe our ideas of the dignity of the individual as the image of God, and the sanctity of human life. It underlies our belief that we are free and responsible, not merely the victims of necessity and chance. And if we think of society as the place where we realise a vision of the good, somewhere behind that thought lies the influence of Exodus and Deuteronomy and Amos and Isaiah.

But one of the most powerful assumptions of the twentieth century is that faith is not like that. It belongs to private life. Religion and society are two independent entities, so that we can edit God out of the language and leave our social world unchanged. After all, the whole history of the modern mind has been marked by the progressive detachment of knowledge from religious tradition. We no longer need, nor would we even think of invoking, God in order to understand nature or history. That battle was fought and lost by religion in the nineteenth century. But if what we know about ourselves and the world is independent of God, what difference could it make whether or not we still had religious faith? It might make all the difference to the private mind of the believer, but in the public world in which we act and interact, it should make no difference at all.

It was in the 1960s that we discovered how false this was.

It was then that radical theologians took perverse pleasure in reciting that God – at least as we had known Him – was dead. But far from making no difference, that made a very great difference indeed. Because it was just then, in the decade of doing your own thing, that morality began to seem simply a matter of personal choice. A moral revolution was announced. In 1967, Sir Edmund Leach began his Reith Lectures with the words, 'Men have become gods. Isn't it about time we understood our own divinity?' A massive shift was taking place in our public culture. Something was lost which we have not yet replaced. Faith and society turned out to be connected after all. If the idea of God was in eclipse, so was the way of life which it served as a foundation. The biblical tradition and its hierarchy of values had lost their persuasive power. And for a moment, rather than lament the fact, we enjoyed our liberation.

The sixties were probably the last time revolution could be sung to so cheerful a tune. Since then we have become increasingly aware of some of the problems of our social ecology: the urban slums, pollution, broken families and residual poverty which seem to yield neither to the welfare state nor to the minimalist state. We are less sure than we were that the future will be better than the past, that economic growth is open-ended or that Utopia can be brought by any sort of revolution. So long as confidence in human progress remained high, religious belief seemed a dispensable commodity. But that optimism has now been shattered. Technology, which seemed to give man godlike powers of creation, has given him also demonic possibilities for destruction. Our loss of a shared morality has fragmented our social world and made even our most intimate relationships seem fragile and conditional. The question is: what moral resources have we left to lend us faith in difficult times? And the answer surely is: far fewer in Fukuyama's consumer culture than there are in the biblical tradition. We cannot edit God out of the language and leave our social world unchanged.

But is Britain yet a post-religious society? Suppose that you had just landed in Britain for the first time and you wanted to know whether you had arrived in a religious country. What signs would you see? You would certainly see some. Here and there you would notice large religious buildings, mainly churches and cathedrals, whose intricate grandeur suggested considerable prestige. You would discover that religious leaders, bishops in particular, were quoted in the newspapers and sat in the House of Lords. You would be struck by the fact that a large number of businesses stopped on Sunday and, asking why, would receive an explanation that could hardly fail to mention Christianity. You might stop to ask why so many people were called John or David or Sarah or Elizabeth and you would learn that these were originally figures in the Bible. Enquiring, you would find that four in five Britons still regard themselves as Christian, that there are ethnic minorities where different traditions are still strong, and that only a tiny minority of the population describe themselves as atheists or agnostics. You might conclude that you had arrived in a religious society.

But you could hardly fail to notice different indicators as well. Examining the city skyline, you might well suspect that the true cathedrals of the urban landscape are office blocks. You would notice that the arenas where crowds gathered and formed temporary communions were football matches and pop concerts. You would see far fewer people engaged in spiritual exercises than in physical exercises. And if you came across individuals in solitary meditation, they would probably be watching a video rather than reading the *Book of Common Prayer*.

You might be perplexed that so many churches had so few people in them; that there were urban areas where fewer than one in a hundred attended church on Sunday. And you would be struck by the fact that the largest crowds visiting cathedrals were tourists, not worshippers. Religion might be, in Stevie Smith's words, not waving but drowning.

What would you make of it all? You would, I think, rightly conclude that these survivals of religion were just that: survivals, residues of an earlier age in which religious institutions played a far greater part in our culture than they do today. But you might notice this as well. That places of worship weren't quite yet museums. Inside them, you weren't an observer or spectator only. You participated. They were perhaps the one place left where you stood in a living relationship with the past.

How is it, then, that religion, that was so central a component of the culture of the past, has come to be so marginal in the present? It is a story part-intellectual, part-social. There was the rise of experimental science in the seventeenth century, the discovery that you could find out more about the world by observing it and framing hypotheses that could be tested, than by relying on past traditions: what Don Cupitt calls the shift from myths to maths. There were the revolutionary changes in the way human beings were perceived: Spinoza's insistence that man, too, is a part of nature and subject to its laws. Marx's suggestion that our ideas are the product of economic forces, and Darwin's discovery that, as someone once put it, man's family tree goes back to the time when his ancestors were swinging from it. Individually, these weakened the hold of the narrative in the first chapter of Genesis in which man was created in the image of God. Collectively, they suggested the power of free enquiry as against the authority of ancient texts, when it came to the pursuit of knowledge.

The biblical tradition, far from being able to stand aside from these developments, eventually came under their scrutiny. Once thinkers were able to distance themselves from religion's claims, they were able to see it as a phenomenon to be explained like any other, in terms of economics or psychology, the projection on to heaven of human interests and needs. The supernatural had a natural explanation, and this weakened the idea of a divine intrusion into the human domain, immune to the relativities of time. The ideas, central to the Bible, of revelation, miracle and redemption were undermined.

And these intellectual developments went hand in hand with a transformation of society. It was difficult to see truth as timeless when the world was embarked on a roller-coaster of change. The industrial revolution broke up old crafts and communities and the traditions that went with them. And it changed the way people began to think about religion's most potent domain: ethics, or how to behave. An ethic which took science as its model would focus not on precedent but on consequences. Actions, like hypotheses, could be tested, and the best were those that produced the greatest happiness for the greatest number. All this meant a quite tangible shift in the direction of human thought, from past to future, from essence to function, from virtue to pragmatism, and from passivity to control. Not only were the communities disrupted in which religious traditions had been lived and transmitted, but the entire cast of mind in which biblical ideas found a home had now gone. Consciousness had been secularised.

And throughout it all, with few dissenting voices, the consensus was that it was a journey of moral progress. But, as they used to say in Yiddish: if things are so good, how come they are so bad? Because our modern conviction that man is part of nature, subject to its laws, is much more like paganism than the biblical view of human dignity. The idea, which has gained great power in recent decades, that human life is dispensable through abortion or euthanasia looks more like a regression than a moral advance. And the notion that authenticity means making our own rules, is the loss of a world of value beyond the self. Wasn't the crucial biblical insight that something else might be true? That man, gifted with language and thus imagination, might seek meaning in the midst of chaos and come to experience it in the form of a moral call not implicit within nature, but beyond? We might well feel that the whole thrust of the scientific imagination when applied to human culture was not so much to elevate man to the status of a god, but to reduce him to the quintessence of dust, and brand all else an illusion. If so, we would have had our first intimation that what seemed so liberating about a post-religious age might be no more than a narrowing of human possibilities.

But only the first. For the fact, almost too obvious to need re-stating, is that not only have technological societies not replaced religious belief with some new overarching canopy of meaning. But in principle they could not do so. The very growth of modern knowledge has come about through specialisation and compartmentalisation, so that an integrated universe linking man and the cosmos is now beyond us. The more we know collectively, the less we know individually. Each of us understands very little of our world.

Not only that. The productive and social changes of the last two centuries have vastly multiplied our choices. Long gone are the days when our identities, beliefs and life chances were narrowly circumscribed by where and to whom we happened to be born. We are no longer actors in a play written by tradition and directed by community, in which roles are allocated by accidents of birth. Instead, careers, relationships and lifestyles have become thing we freely choose from a superstore of alternatives.

Modernity is the transition from fate to choice. At the same time it dissolves the commitments and loyalties that once lay behind our choices. Technical reason has made us masters of matching means to ends. But it has left us inarticulate as to why we should choose one end rather than another. The values that once led us to regard one as intrinsically better than another, and which gave such weight to words like good and bad, have disintegrated, along with the communities and religious traditions in which we learned them. Now we choose because we choose. Because it is what we want; or it works for us; or it feels right to me. Once we have dismantled a world in which larger virtues held sway, what is left are success and self-expression, the key values of an individualistic culture.

But can a society survive on so slender a moral base? It is a question that was already raised in the nineteenth century by figures like Alexis de Tocqueville and Max Weber, who saw most clearly the connection between modern liberal democracies and JudaeoChristian tradition. It was de Tocqueville who saw that religion tempered individualism and gave those engaged in the competitive economy a capacity for benevolence and self-sacrifice.

And it was he who saw that this was endangered by the very pursuit of affluence that was the key to economic growth. Max Weber delivered the famous prophetic warning that the cloak of material prosperity might eventually become an iron cage. It was already becoming an end in itself, and other values were left, in his words, 'like the ghost of dead religious beliefs'. Once capitalism consumed its religious foundations, both men feared the consequences.

The stresses of a culture without shared meanings are already mounting, and we have yet to count the human costs. We see them in the move from a morality of self-imposed restraint to one in which we increasingly rely on law to protect us from ourselves. In the past, disadvantaged groups could find in religion what Karl Marx called 'the feeling of a heartless world'. A purely economic order offers no such consolations. A culture of success places little value on the unsuccessful.

The erosion of those bonds of loyalty and love which religion undergirded has left us increasingly alone in an impersonal economic and social system. Emile Durkheim was the first to give this condition a name. He called it *anomie*: the situation in which individuals have lost their moorings in a collective order. It is the heavy price we pay for our loss of communities of faith.

Fukuyama described a future dedicated to 'economic calculation, the endless solving of technical problems . . . and the satisfaction of sophisticated consumer demands'. But is such a world socially viable? Not all human problems are technical.

One, above all, is not: the search for meaning which gave rise to the religious imagination in the first place.

I have called the biblical tradition part of our moral ecology, by which I mean that until recently the language of British and American politics was rich in biblical themes: covenant and kinship, exodus and liberation, human dignity and responsibility. A religious vision could inspire Edmund Burke to conservatism, William Cobbett to socialism, and wend its variations from Thomas Jefferson to Martin Luther King. At times it spoke of the duty of the state to the individual, at others of the freedom of the individual against the state. It was a language, not a party political programme. But it was a distinctive language, quite unlike the vocabulary of a consumer culture, in which we speak only of rights and entitlements, interests and choices, self-expression and success. It referred to meanings beyond the self, to moral communities beyond the individual and to relationships more enduring than temporary compatibility. It was a language that linked private faith to public action. It brought together what modernity has split asunder: society and the self. It was this tradition that led the great Talmudist, Rabbi Hayyim of Brisk, to define the role of a religious leader as, 'to redress the grievances of those who are abandoned and alone, to protect the dignity of the poor, and to save the oppressed from the hands of his oppressor'. It moved one of Judaism's greatest mystics, the Rabbi of Kotzk, to say that someone else's material concerns are my spiritual concerns.

But it is just this that leads me to believe that Fukuyama's prediction has not yet come to pass. For we still see other people's suffering and poverty not as things that merely happen as part of an impersonal order, but as things we ought somehow to relieve. And, for so long as we do so, we have moved beyond a view of society as just the free play of interests. It remains a moral enterprise, actualising its values through history; the end point of which is redemption or, in Aaron Lichtenstein's fine phrase, collective beatitude. We are back in the language of justice and compassion, words we once learned from the Bible and which led us to construct the society we have.

Which leads in turn to a significant conclusion: that, though our churches and synagogues are under-attended, people have not stopped identifying themselves as religious individuals; nor have they yet stopped thinking in religious ways. However attenuated, the attachments remain. And this means more than that religion is for us a matter of nostalgia, or habit, or memories of grandparents and a simpler way of life. It means that it still remains for us a possibility.

We are capable of being moved by calls to our conscience, to acts that make no sense in terms of self-fulfilment or private ambition. We have not yet lost the language of older and larger visions of the shared redemptive enterprise. We have it because the biblical tradition survives in our culture-marginal, endangered, a survival to be sure, but still there. Reminding us that the rules we make are subject to the rules we didn't make, and that the making of moral history is not yet at an end.

1986

John McCluskey

～

Law, Justice and Democracy

Extract from 'Hard Cases and Bad Law'

Lord McCluskey (1929–2017), was a Scottish lawyer, judge and politician. His lecture series discussed the role of the judiciary. In his third lecture, he argues that Parliament, not the judiciary, must have ultimate responsibility for the legislation, arguing that they must not abdicate the making of policy choices to 'a body of elderly men'.

In deciding the cases that come before them, judges can and do make law, and Parliament is free to accept that judge-made law or to alter it. If Parliament chooses to legislate, then there can, at least in theory, be no conflict between the law made by Parliament and the law applied in the courts. And if anyone wants to assert that the law made by Parliament is of an inferior metal, then the one audience that will not listen to that argument is the judiciary.

But if we are to consider allowing the validity of laws enacted by Parliament to be challenged in the courts on the ground of supposed conflict with some fundamental or supreme law; if we are to think of allowing the judges' solutions, based upon their interpretation of an entrenched charter of fundamental law, to prevail over those of Parliament, then perhaps we ought first to give some thought to the character of law made by judges. I shall look at one field of law in which the courts were immensely creative and in which the judge-made law inevitably affected the lives of millions who had no part in the making of that law, little knowledge of its content, and no freedom to contract out of it: the field of law governing the rights of injured persons to recover damages in respect of accidental injury. Unlike many other areas of the law, such as those concerned with commercial contracts or wills, it was not practicable for most of the people affected by the law to study the judge-made rules with a view to modifying their behaviour so as to fit it within the rules.

The fundamental notion that judges developed to govern the making of reparation for accidental injury was the notion of wrong, of some fault, some blameworthiness on the part of an identified wrongdoer who could be made subject to the effective jurisdiction of the court and so be made to pay any damages found due. This is an individualistic and moralistic notion. It means that injury itself gives no right to compensation: the person who has done the injury must be identified and sued. The wrongdoer must be arraigned before the court, not to be punished but to be ordered to compensate in money. The victim must obtain evidence to establish that the alleged wrongdoer has been guilty of a wrongful act which caused the injury. It is not enough that another's act has caused your injury. It has to be shown that that act was in breach of some duty that the law recognised as apt to create rights and obligations. Because there had to be proof by acceptable evidence of all the essentials, the victim had to have the economic capacity, and the will, to gather the evidence, to finance the litigation, to endure, if necessary, the extra legal sanctions that the alleged wrongdoer was free to deploy – such as the threat of dismissal from employment – as well as the capacity to wait, perhaps for years, for the case to be concluded. There was inevitably the risk of failure, but even an apparent success could sometimes be rendered hollow by the deduction of legal expenses incurred on the road to that success.

And there were other formidable obstacles. Contributory negligence, the judges decided, was a complete bar to success: and the employer was not held responsible when one employee negligently injured another; each employee was required to take the risk of his fellow servant's negligence, a judge-made doctrine which, though gradually modified, left a considerable gap in the rights of employed persons. Other claims were defeated by the development of the doctrine that certain people must be deemed to have voluntarily accepted risks to which they were exposed. And, by creating particular immunities, the judges erected other barriers to the recovery of compensation. So the pursuit of compensation was a game of Snakes and Ladders, a lottery in which the innocence or the hurt of the victim was no guarantee of success. Some innocent victims recovered damages. Others did not. The chances of landing on a snake were so feared that even those who were able to make a substantial claim could seldom take the risk of a fight to the finish to obtain their whole rights. Most cases were compromised on the principle that a bird in the hand was worth three in the thicket. And even with its successes, limited though they were, the judge-made law did little, if anything, to reduce the risk of injury. The courts could take no steps to attack the causes of industrial injury: it would have been difficult for judges so to develop their powers as to compel the introduction of safer working practices, to secure the performance of duty rather than just a payment for its breach.

It would have been even more difficult for judges to develop a system whereby the payment of compensation depended on the need of the injured person rather than upon the responsibility of a wrongdoer; because litigation in the civil courts is concerned with vindicating the rights of one citizen at the expense of another. If the plaintiff wins damages it is because the defendant must pay them. The idea that a plaintiff could win a right to compensation without somebody being held responsible to pay it just did not make sense in a court of law. Judges could not create a fund to enable compensation to be paid to those among the injured or bereaved who could not pin the blame upon a solvent wrongdoer. In a court, the idea of no-fault compensation was unthinkable. Judges could not reach out from the necessary limitations of the system in order to confer rights to compensation based upon need.

The judges who, over a long period of time, made such law, and then applied it, were certainly not operating in one of the law's unimportant backwaters. It was an area in which many people made their only contact with the law, and for many such people that contact was all-important. If the law allowed no redress for being blinded or crippled and gave no compensation, then they would look in vain elsewhere.

What are we to make of the body of law that the judges created? Though most people would agree that incoherence, illogicality and irrationality would be serious defects in the

JOHN MCCLUSKEY

law, few would say that the law was good just because it was coherent, logical and based on a clear principle. Judges will very properly aim for these qualities. But in themselves, even when achieved, they do not make the law good. The law can be considered good only if, being coherent, predictable and principled, it also produces results which are socially acceptable. And the results of the judge-made law in the field of reparation for personal injury left too much to be desired. For too many there was, and is still, no remedy.

Tickets in a lottery

For those for whom the law could provide a remedy, the route to it was slow, expensive, hazardous and uncertain. Even from the defendant's point of view, the law was unsatisfactory. The cost of litigation was high. Insuring against the risks of litigation became very high. It has recently become clear – especially in America, where generally the same legal principles apply – that the fear of being sued, and the cost of insuring against that risk, have begun to make serious inroads into the availability of vital public services, including medical treatment. When the law, properly applied, produces the result that those who need medical treatment cannot have it because doctors are afraid of being sued, then it produces a result which is not socially acceptable.

If we end up, as we do, with a body of law which affords

remedies which too often have the appearance of tickets in a lottery, which threatens to inhibit the provision of medical care or other necessary services and which hardly serves to raise standards of care, then it is little wonder that some countries have decided to abandon the whole judge-made edifice and introduce no-fault compensation.

It would be wrong to suggest that there was no rhyme or reason to it all; there was. It was not necessarily the logic of the judges that was to blame; it was the major premises that preceded the adjudication. And quite apart from the constitutional inability of our courts to reach out and introduce positive measures designed to achieve social justice, the very nature of litigation and of judicial training are such that judges cannot calculate or control the long-term effects of the law, which they build up painstakingly, one decision at a time. In the United States Supreme Court, judges can, and do, select and assemble a whole spectrum of real cases to be considered at the one time and can hear representations not just from the interested parties but from others who are concerned about the consequences for the law of whatever ruling is made. So the judges obtain briefings about the social and economic results of formulating the law in a particular way before deciding what the policy of the law is to be. But once judges do that, they have ceased to be judges as we know them. They have become legislators making informed policy choices.

I do not believe that our judges can or should be given

such tools, or such a role. It is not a role which, by tradition, training or experience they are qualified to perform. When we ask judges to decide the legal rights and wrongs of litigants we are doing something for which there is no tenable alternative. Someone must resolve the disputes. It has to be judges. And there is no escape from using, as judges, lawyers whose mental equipment includes assumptions and prejudgments which lie outside the letter of the law. Equally, we have to accept that as they decide one case after another, some of these very assumptions and prejudgments become part of the law, as much, indeed, as if they had been enacted by Parliament.

In a common-law tradition like ours, the judges have to fill the gaps and make law. But let us be clear that that is what they are doing. Let us understand that society, if it does not review the provisional, the necessary, the imperfect law made by judges, is abdicating the making of its policy choices to what Lord Devlin called 'a body of elderly men'. It is the proper function of governments and democratically elected legislators to consider and make policy choices, not the proper function of judges.

That in itself is no startling or revolutionary proposition. On the contrary, it has been accepted in modern times that an activist Parliament must intervene in order to remake or restate the law which has been evolved by judges, and Parliament must fulfil that role not just when the whole thrust of the judge-made law has produced results which are notoriously seen to be no longer socially acceptable. It must do so at all times to grapple with the classic problem of law in society; the difficulty, some would say the impossibility, of writing down the law so that it is certain and its application predictable, while at the same time ensuring that it prescribes and achieves a fair and just result in individual cases.

It is, for the most part, the courts, the judges, that have to resolve the so-called 'hard cases', the cases in which the law points to a result which appears to be unfair, or the cases in which different principles or rules of law clash and compel a choice, a choice which determines the result. This problem can, of course, arise whether the existing law has been enacted by Parliament or created by judges. It will commonly arise if, when the law was laid down, the particular problem was not foreseen, perhaps because it could not have been foreseen.

Thus, for example, the law which defined adultery and held it to be a matrimonial offence, giving rise to certain rights in the innocent spouse, had settled down and appeared to be comprehensively defined and understood, until science discovered a way of impregnating a woman artificially with the semen of a man whom she had never met. Until then the law was quite simple. If a man had lived completely apart from his wife for a year and then discovered she was pregnant he could divorce her on the ground of adultery; the law would hold the pregnancy to be sufficient evidence of adultery, and there could be no answer. Then science provided an answer. The wife, in a particular case, could say: 'I haven't committed

adultery; I have been made pregnant by artificial insemin-
ation.' Today, she might go further and say: 'I have hired out
my womb for a fee and am merely a host for someone else's
fertilised ovum.' So, for the first time, lawyers have to decide
if physical intercourse is the essential feature of adultery, or
whether adultery is committed when a wife conceives a child
of which her husband is not the father.

A judge faced with such a question cannot sidestep it by
saying: 'This is an unforeseen and unprovided-for situation;
let Parliament deal with it.' He has to decide, and some
new law is made. Obviously, most advances in technology
are capable of throwing up unforeseen problems for which
the existing law does not provide and the old law has to be
stretched by judges to furnish answers which will fill the gaps
until Parliament attempts to fashion a legal structure to regulate the rights and responsibilities of those affected by the new
state of facts. But even without the trigger of technological
innovation, gradual changes in the perception of what is fair
and reasonable can suggest that the old law is inadequate, and
cause judges to nurture new principles and limit old ones in
order to impose restrictions or make available remedies that
were not available before.

This happened in relation to the concept of cruelty in
matrimonial cases, in which the judges gradually departed
from the idea that such cruelty had to be physical, and allowed
divorce for mental cruelty. Likewise, in the field of public
order, the courts responded to unwelcomed forms of protest

by adapting the concept of breach of the peace, and the unfairness of the judge-made doctrine of common employment led later judges to modify its excesses; though, until Parliament intervened, the law remained unjust.

Elusive Definitions

The so-called 'hard cases' in which the justice of the case leads to one result, though the existing law points to another, do not always produce bad law in the sense that the particular results are unfair; but they tend to produce uncertain law. Law which is uncertain is bad in principle, even if the results in particular cases can be justified. When long-standing rules can be abandoned, when too many cases divide judicial opinion and can be decided either way, then the warning signals should be out.

Yet despite the wisdom of the judges, despite their independence, despite their impartiality, their traditions, their analytical skills, they disagree about what the law is or should be. Such disagreement is unlikely to flow from overt political preferences. It flows from the fact that where there is uncertainty, there is bound to be disagreement. Unanimity is a rare phenomenon when there is room for doubt, and the law, even today, contains a surprisingly large number of grey areas.

That is true even in the criminal law: the recent report of the Fraud Trials Committee, sitting under the chairmanship of Lord Roskill, illustrates that even an apparently simple concept like dishonesty is one that the law and judges, at least in England, cannot readily explain to juries. And a recent well-known case demonstrates a similar phenomenon. The case is *Regina v Hancock & Another*, the case of the two striking Welsh miners who killed a taxi driver by dropping concrete on his taxi as he drove another miner to work. The facts were simple enough, but the critical question was whether the two miners had acted with what the law would recognise as murderous intent. That looks like a question of fact. But the trial judge explained the law about intent in such terms that after some five hours the jury sent a note to the judge indicating that they were perplexed. So the judge gave them further directions in law. If they were puzzled the first time, the second direction would not have helped them, because the trial judge just repeated to the jury what he had said the first time. That is hardly surprising, because he was being extremely careful to give the jury exactly the directions which had been prescribed by the House of Lords itself only a short time before in the case of Maloney. The jury brought in a verdict of murder against the two miners. On appeal, the Court of Appeal quashed the conviction for murder and substituted a verdict of manslaughter. They did so on the ground that what the trial judge had said was potentially misleading: in other words that the House of Lords had got it wrong in the earlier (Maloney) case.

So the Crown appealed to the Lords, who had then to decide if the guidelines they had laid down in Maloney's case were sound or defective. They agreed that the guidelines laid down in Maloney's case were defective, but they disagreed with the Court of Appeal's suggestions as to what the guidelines ought to be in future cases. Exactly where that leaves the trial judge in future cases has yet to be seen. But it must be a matter for some dismay that in 1985 and 1986 the judges in the highest courts were still at sixes and sevens as to the appropriate formulation of the guidance to be given to juries on a matter as basic, as common and as elementary as intent in a murder case. There is something wrong when, after considering hundreds of criminal cases involving intent, we still cannot produce an agreed and universally accepted statement of precisely what the law requires for proof of specific intent.

No one can criticise the jury in the Hancock case. There is a tendency, which is by no means new, to claim that juries cannot be trusted to handle complex criminal cases. But if the Hancock saga is evidence of anything, it is that the problem is not in the jury but in the remarkable difficulty that judges have in determining and explaining the legal principles and rules which juries have to apply.

The Lamp of Freedom

The inevitable result of reducing the role of the jury would be to increase the role of the judge, so it is worth glancing at the other half of that remarkable forensic partnership.

The jury is not one unvarying institution, possessing the same character and powers wherever it is found. Juries vary in size from six to fifteen members. They decide civil and criminal cases. Sometimes they have to be unanimous; sometimes they are allowed to deliver a verdict by a simple or a qualified majority. They mostly resolve issues of fact, but sometimes must decide mixed questions of fact and law. In some jurisdictions they may have a role in the sentencing process, as well as in determining guilt or innocence. The nature of the right to a jury trial in a criminal case varies in different countries.

I have no wish to provide an index to all varieties of the jury. It would be substantial. I merely want to caution against the insular notion that the jury is an institution as unvarying in time and character as the Rock of Ages. It is not, even when it is embedded, as in America, in a constitution. It is a tool with many different uses and dimensions.

The use of juries has had a profound effect upon court procedures and rules of evidence. Juries came to cases totally ignorant of the background; some jurors could not read. So the trial took the form of an oral presentation of the facts, with both sides having carefully defined rights to present and to challenge evidence before an open-minded court. Neither judge nor jury had an inquisitorial role. The rules of evidence were fashioned to ensure that juries heard nothing that might prejudice their consideration of the narrow issues they had to resolve, and the jury sat mute until it pronounced the winners and the losers.

Learned commentators, here and in America, compared the form of litigation resulting from the use of juries to a sporting contest, a boxing match, a fox-hunt. Lord Devlin expressed the more traditional view in describing the criminal jury system as 'the lamp of freedom . . . the beacon that seven centuries have tended'. Lord Denning said it was 'the best guarantee of our freedoms'. I agree with that. But it is best to see the jury as it is: an imperfect instrument in an imperfect world, an instrument fashioned by history, rather than by any very conscious design, an instrument that takes on a local colour in different jurisdictions.

So what are we to make of Lord Devlin's assertion that if there were a tyrant in Whitehall his first object would be to make Parliament utterly subservient to his will, and the next to overthrow or diminish trial by jury? Since he spoke, the Diplock courts have replaced jury trials in Northern Ireland in relation to offences from murder downwards, and, after public calls by some judges, the Fraud Trials Committee, under the chairmanship of Lord Roskill, has proposed that for certain fraud cases trial by tribunal should replace trial by jury. These and other changes certainly diminish trial by jury. So are there tyrants in Whitehall? I hope not. I think it is going too far to suggest that simply altering the jury system is necessarily a giant leap towards tyranny. If it were, then Scotland – where there is no automatic right to a jury trial in most cases, and where juries can return a verdict by a simple majority – must have been in the grip of tyrants for centuries.

Too many lawyers take a patronising view of juries. For myself, I have prosecuted and defended in complex fraud, corruption and other such trials in Scotland, with jurors selected from the voters' roll, with some of the jurors almost as young as the accused in the dock and some almost as old as the judge on the bench, without ever feeling that the jury failed to understand by the end what the point was. We should not patronise jurors by regarding them as too young, too old, too immature or too stupid to understand how an accused person has brought about some definite practical result by false pretences. If it really were true that jurors could not, after hearing the evidence, understand the types of fraud case listed in the Roskill report, then they really have no business to be deciding about murder, rape and arson. If there is something wrong with the way in which those who perpetrate frauds are brought to justice, or are not brought to justice, then the probability is that those who investigate such frauds are not up to the task and those who present the cases to the jury are unable to see the wood for the trees.

I am not persuaded that the system for establishing the guilt or innocence of those charged with complex fraud or any other serious crime has broken down. And if it is showing signs of stress then I consider that those who lay the blame on the jury are firing at the wrong target. If we are to trim the wick of the lamp of freedom, let us do it on the basis of evidence that it is necessary, not just because some people suppose that judges could make a better job of determining guilt or innocence than a large body of properly instructed citizens sitting as jurors. What has to be done is to simplify the law, to improve the facilities for juries, to humanise court rituals and modernise rules of evidence, and to devise ways to ensure that the cases are presented to juries in a manner that is worthy of the high intellectual competence and substantial remuneration of the lawyers, including judges, who take part in such trials.

Of course juries sometimes acquit people who probably have committed the crimes with which they have been charged. But the principal reason for that is that under our law no person can be convicted of a crime unless his guilt is established beyond reasonable doubt, upon the basis of admissible evidence. I would not for one moment suggest that we should tamper with the burden or the standard of proof. I ask merely that we acknowledge that it is that standard, and not the gullibility of jurors, that secures acquittals in most of those cases in which the prosecution fails. If it happens too often that the guilty go free, let us rather re-examine the rules and procedures, to see if in a civilised society we can properly provide the jury with more pieces of the jigsaw of truth.

I am not sure if the current criticisms of the criminal jury system and how it is seen to operate spring from the same attitudes that cause some lawyers to wax lyrical about the new activism of judges in judicial review and urge the dramatic change in the scope and character of judicial review that enacting a Bill of Rights would effect. Certainly, diminishing the role of the jury while enlarging that of the judge would achieve a significant shift of power in the whole field of public order. And obviously, to diminish the system of trial by jury and at the same time to enact a Bill of Rights is to engage judges in highly visible activities, all related to law, order, justice and freedom.

What I question is the true relevance of such changes to the real problems of order and justice. To enact a Bill of Rights in noble language and to set judges to apply it to cases would, I suspect, be the modern equivalent of writing and producing a morality play. It would be entertaining, even instructive, and would allow us to applaud the occasional triumph of those values that the scriptwriters favoured. But it would have little effect on how people behaved in the real world.

1978

A. H. Halsey

Change in British Society

Extract from 'The Social Order'

Dr Albert Henry Halsey (1923–2014), was a British sociologist and professor at the University of Oxford. His Reith Lecture series explored a sociological perspective on contemporary Britain. In his final lecture, he explains how societies are made through cohesion in group interests, but societies are also broken by arguments and competition. He analyses how the authoritative power of the state presides over its society.

It is perfectly possible that the United Kingdom of England, Scotland, Wales and Northern Ireland will shortly disintegrate. Even to say this in 1978 may be thought sacrilegious: and to have said it ten years ago would have to be dismissed as absurd. But I must immediately point out that, if, for a moment, we look beyond our native pieties and take, instead, the wider perspective of contemporary world history, the prospect of our approaching insular disestablishment is rather commonplace. Integration between nations, and ethnic disintegration within them, is the common pattern of current economic and political development all over the world. We find ourselves drawn simultaneously into the European Economic Community and into Scottish and Welsh separatism. The very different political and economic circumstances of the Russian empire, of China, and of Africa, reveal, on a larger scale in each case, the same story. Enlarging economic organisation, with modernity as its aim, combines with sharp internal conflicts between Russian and non-Russian within the USSR, Han and non-Han minorities in China, and tribal groups in Africa. Our own experience is not unique. Nor is conflict, despite our cultural bias against recognising it, in any way odd. The coexistence of interests and scarcity makes it more difficult to explain why societies hang together, rather than why they break up.

All the more, then, is it a puzzle that, at least since Culloden in 1746, and despite historical rumours about 1688, 1848 and 1926, and notwithstanding the southern Irish breakaway in 1922, and the current so-called 'troubles' which we hesitate to name as civil war, British history and the British state have been quite outstandingly tranquil. Ever since the battles between the parliamentary armies and the forces of the crown, more than 300 years ago, the outstanding fact about Britain is domestic peace.

Why? How did the nation that led the industrial revolution somehow contrive this changelessness? How did it retain monarchic and mediaeval symbols of unity, absorb first a bourgeoisie, and second a proletariat, turn Hadrian's Wall and the Edward castles into tourist attractions, and contain the eisteddfod (which, I am told, is a mediaeval invention of the nineteenth century) and the kilt as quaint, atavistic, regional colourfulness, signifying politically nothing? And why, if it is so, are these ancient manifestations of war, bloodshed, force and oppression, so long turned into harmless symbols of pacification and gentleness, now re-emerging as signals of separatism and hostility? These are the questions for my final talk: the problem of fraternity which has been latent in my discussion of liberty and equality, the problem of social order which has underlain my chronicle of class, status and party.

One thing is obvious. Neither Marxism nor liberalism

can solve our central problem – the problem of order or, as I have put it, fraternity. Neither tradition ever developed a serious theory of nationalism. For the Marxist, nationalism is a secondary force, more or less useful in the march of history towards world revolution, given greater or lesser emphasis, according to whether the theorist prefers Lenin or Rosa Luxemburg. Liberal theory, too, has a central concept of one world, evolving, as rationality displaces mercantilism and other superstitions, towards free trade, patterned by comparative cost advantages. Both theories come out of the early development of capitalism, both vastly overestimate the possibility of economic solutions: the Marxists, by assuming that the economic power of the capitalist class is all that stands in the way of a harmonious society of free and equal men, needing no political state to organise their brotherhood; the liberals, by assuming that the free market generates just distribution, needing only minimal government to guard its contractual perfection.

I want to argue that there are native traditions of social and political theory which can be of more use to us in our search for a solution. If the first enemy of social peace in Britain is the persistence of inequality, then we can look to such writers as T. H. Marshall who avoids both the Marxist and the liberal error.

Societies are made and broken by like interests leading to cohesion or competition, and by unlike interests which bind men together or bring them into conflict. But there is another principle of social organisation – domination – which has become increasingly important in modern societies in the form of the authority of rationally created rules. Authority always has two sides, force and faith: the faith of the ruled that the rulers have the right to make rules by which people must live (for example, that they must pay so much in taxes); and the force that the rulers have at their disposal to compel compliance with the rules. In modern societies, by far the most important source of authoritative rules is the state, and the definition of the state, at once most simple and most useful, is that it has a monopoly of ultimate force in the territory it claims. But societies are not identical with states, as the example of Scotland clearly shows.

The integration of a society is based less on force and more on faith; that is, on cultural affinities of language, custom, belief and history which give the members a consciousness of kind and kin with each other and a sense of cultural boundary from other peoples. These bonds are more enduring, so that states and empires have risen and fallen more rapidly than have societies: a nation and people can live, politically or militarily speaking, underground, through many generations of foreign rule. Faith converts force into authority and consent. At all events, force and faith, in their varied manifestations, have played their part in what has been, historically, a remarkably united kingdom. Some of the unifying influences are easy enough to discern. The British state, centred on the monarch in Parliament, held undisputed sway over England,

Scotland and Wales for centuries and, more important, naval power controlled an empire eventually covering one-quarter of the land surface of the whole earth. Britain, in 1900, was still the greatest of imperial nations, a major workshop of the world, and miraculously secured at the same time by a still impregnable insularity. British society was itself the apex of a worldwide imperial dominion, and London the financial centre of world trade.

This powerful combination of industry and empire obviously afforded huge wealth and wide opportunity to its controllers. Wealth and opportunity were most unequally shared within the society, between classes, sexes and regions. But continuing, if decelerating and unsteady, expansion, itself a supplement to integration, was further and massively reinforced by the custom and culture of a most peculiar island. It was a culture of patrician liberalism. The aristocracy and the gentry maintained a dominance over both society and state, from the overthrow of absolutist monarchy, in the seventeenth century, and right through the imperial and industrial development of the next 200 years.

Liberalism, as a theory of free markets in the service of economic growth, is older in England than the bourgeois industrialist manufacturer. The English landowning classes had developed it long before the industrial revolution. The aristocracy and the gentry absorbed the bourgeoisie in the nineteenth century. This gave the twentieth century a stratified society which, though strongly resembling the Marxist description of polarised class society if one looked at the northern industrial towns, was also a status hierarchy of apparent agelessness. It was rooted in a mediaeval agrarian past. It provided a governing class descended from preindustrial times to which was added, especially in the southern counties, those whose wealth and status derived from the empire, and from the finance capitalism of the City of London.

In short, Edwardian Britain was a country of inequality, but a strongly knit nation. In the course of overseas imperialism and domestic industrialisation, a legacy of feudal aristocracy had been accepted by both bourgeoisie and proletariat. No wonder, then, that Lord David Cecil saw the sunset over his grandfather's deathbed as also the twilight of British greatness, for the fusion I have briefly sketched was gradually to be undone by its frailties at home and abroad. Abroad, the industrial competitors – America and Germany – had already ended Britain's primacy. In a century of relative, though not absolute, decline, there was a period of prosperity in the 1950s and '60s. When that interlude ended, publicly bewailed economic stagnation, class and status inequalities and, more recently, the recrudescence of older nationalisms were less and less easily contained by the traditional remedies of political liberalism, gentlemanly culture and civic incorporation.

Nevertheless, there have been strong forces making for integration. If only because we are so accustomed now to gloomy discussion of economic decline, we should remind ourselves that this century has been one of economic growth.

A. H. HALSEY

The average person is unquestionably better fed, better clothed, better housed, and enjoys a longer, healthier and more leisured life than his Edwardian predecessor. Clearly, allegiance to a society is more secure when these ameliorations are in train; that is, when the generations see a darker past and a brighter future.

We also do well to remind ourselves of the integrating aspects of war. It is a paradox of external conflict that it promotes equality and fraternity within the nation. Both wars enlarged the horizon of expectations of ordinary men and women, and that erodes fraternity. But the wars also brought renewed promise for the future. They softened class divisions, reduced inequality and reinforced patriotic sentiment.

> Yet ever 'twixt the books and his bright eyes
> The gleaming eagles of the legions came.

This was possible reverie for a young clerk in England in the First World War and even the Second, before the bomb dropped on Hiroshima.

The factor of paramount importance has been the essentially unprincipled inequality of distribution of wealth and income which gives rise to anomy or normlessness. The stubborn persistence of distributional inequality of wealth and income up to 1970 needs no further documentation. And it is true that, at least until recently, the implications of inequality manifested themselves in the economic rather than in the political sphere. Consensual politics have been maintained partly by the remarkably restricted comparisons within and between classes which Runciman has analysed, and partly by the political culture of democracy which I reviewed in my fourth lecture. Within the economic sphere, however – in industrial relations and the management of incomes policy – inequality has been corrosive. The manifestations have not been those of class warfare, but, rather, as John Goldthorpe has argued, 'in a situation of anomy; that is . . . a lack of moral regulation over the wants and goods that individuals hold'.

We must also take account of the fact that the development of the social rights of citizenship generates conflict as well as consensus. The egalitarian principle intrinsic to citizenship challenges normative approval of market inequalities. Class and citizenship are at war in the twentieth century. Citizenship also undermines traditional status hierarchies which, though strongly rooted in British culture, are conventionally, not legally, based. Citizenship is therefore a basis for dissent from the established social order. And the extension of citizenship rights into the industrial sphere – a movement towards various forms of industrial democracy – gives unions and, especially, local groups of workers and their shop stewards increased pro-tection and power to pursue their market and work interests relatively undisciplined by traditional constraints.

So the partial development of the principle of citizenship, under circumstances where competing distributional prin-ciples deriving from class, status and citizenship still contend for pre-eminence, may reduce rather than increase solidarity.

The consequences have been increasingly evident in the recent history of industrial relations. They are most dramatically illustrated in the growing bitterness of race relations in the major English cities.

Our twentieth-century experience has not been one of steady secular decline. Before the First World War, the balance of social solidarity was tipping towards disintegration, mainly along class lines. Class polarisation and alienation from industrial work were growing. These were inevitable features of economic development along capitalist lines, but they were checked in that period by limited working-class expectations and the strong alliance of aristocrat and bourgeois. Meanwhile, the old traditions of civil liberty, in which modern citizenship is rooted, though they provided the legal basis for the development of class inequalities, had also begun to extend into political enfranchisement, and into a set of social rights which later came to be called the welfare state. The organisation of the working class was also built on the same foundations of citizenship. These integrative forces were, however, only weakly struggling into existence. There was also, especially on Clydeside, a serious syndicalist tide flowing away from the more moderate mainstream of the trade unions, the co-operative societies, and the infant Labour Party. The war itself suspended opposition, and brought a primitive form of war socialism, some reduction of wage differentials, and steps towards the emancipation of women.

Return to 'normalcy', as it was then termed, shifted the

balance again towards, but not quite back to, the pre-war situation. Religion had lost some of its restraining power. The expected boundaries of self-fulfilment were pushed back, educational horizons began to widen, and many intellectuals were vehemently critical of bourgeois life and values. This was the period of fellow-travelling.

Nevertheless, this weakening of cultural control never showed signs of being turned into a threatening political movement. British radical politics centred on the Labour Party. Bitter industrial struggles scarred the 1920s, but the rise of the Labour Party after the First World War to replace the Liberal Party was an incorporation in the politics of consensus, not very different from that described in the nineteenth century by Walter Bagehot. And the slump years of the early 1930s temporarily overlaid the basic politics of belief in progress with hopelessness, fatalism and fragmentation – a deadening and defeatist interpretation of events was universally shared: economic depression was seen as externally imposed rather than politically soluble.

Then again, partial recovery and the Second World War eased the tensions and renewed the national promise. Liberty, equality and fraternity all made progress during the war and post-war years. Labour Party philosophy dominated politics, and there were even five early post-war years of a Labour government in clear majority. The following thirteen years of Conservative government were years of full employment, and of educational and occupational opportunity for a significant minority of the new generation of the working class. Belief in an emergent meritocracy was developing in this period, despite the evidence of continuing class inequality of conditions necessary to realise it. It was a time of high net upward mobility, and of slowly burgeoning mass affluence. The tide of political consensus flowed strongly for twenty years or more.

This tide turned yet again in the 1960s. By this time, the empire was gone. Ideologically, all that was left was Powellite English nationalism. Economically, what remained was the overseas-oriented financial capitalism of the City, which drained talent and attention away from the needs of an ageing and sluggish industrial economy. Hope and glory faded from the land. Internal tensions became more anxiously acute with economic stagnation, quickening inflation and rising unemployment.

Meantime, the trade unions, fostered by the further development of citizenship rights, have become more powerfully entrenched, more able to press sectional against national interest. The incorporation of the Labour leadership, both in Parliament and in the TUC, undermined the allegiance of the rank and file, reducing the 'governability' of those officially organised into the working class movement.

There were also ideological movements in these postwar years, with strongly divisive effects. The authority of churches and chapels declined still further. Schoolteachers and parents also became less effective conveyors of cultural values and traditional pieties as they, too, lost confidence in their right and their ability to do so. Scandals, from Profumo in 1963 onwards, dealt repeated blows to the British reputation for incorruptible government. The Poulson revelations of widespread racketeering in the Labour strongholds of the north-east were especially damaging to popular respect for the authority of both the town hall and Whitehall.

There was a marked contrast between the moralistic Primitive Methodist Labour leaders like Peter Lee, and the political bosses like Dan Smith and Andrew Cunningham who replaced them, with their public-relations networks and their eventual exposure and long jail sentences for criminal behaviour in public office. And the adversary culture of students, intellectuals, journalists and media men grew more strident in the 1960s. Then, finally, came the sudden development of serious nationalism in Scotland, echoed by weaker but still significant separatism in Wales. Even the detachment of Northern Ireland became a possibility.

Conclusion

What, then, is the present prospect for British society? There is no simple answer. There are forces of both conflict and cohesion: and they are complex: and they come from the wider world as well as from within our own society. Salvation lies neither in European integration, nor in retreat to the more archaic native nationalisms. These are conditions for successful solutions; they are not the solutions themselves. Nor is there any simple economic answer, whether through North Sea oil or a return to the market. Growth alleviates scarcity. But, at our level of economic development, it stimulates appetite as much as it gratifies it.

Indeed, the greatest danger is precisely the offer of simple solutions to the complexity of our very real plight. We have an economy that does not release our energies, a polity that does not secure our trust, and a culture which does not attract our affections. Simple solutions can only lead back to the barbarism of political tyranny, whether from the right or the left. Either would destroy the one element of our social heritage in which we can take pride – our long developed and tenaciously held civil liberty. Granted all the shortcomings, it remains true that, compared with almost any other society in history, this is the land, as Tennyson said, of old and just renown,

> The land where, girt with friends or foes,
> A man may speak the thing he will.

Our predicament is that the historical conditions which allowed this liberty also permitted hugely divisive inequalities of class and status. They bequeathed us a stratified society held together by imperial might abroad, and deference and respect for shared religious and cultural values at home. But external empire and internal social control have been losing their power to pacify without violence, leaving market success, in all its weakness, to justify a still unequal society.

Our society cannot stand on such shifting foundations. To strengthen them, we need principles and practices of social distribution which are acknowledged to be just by the vast majority. And, in a world of growing visibility of reference groups, these principles will be seen as just only if they are just. The implication is that, in a political democracy, the paramount principle of distribution must be equality. Equality of opportunity is not enough. This is a halfway house we have still not reached, but which is, in any case, along a road towards a society that could be more ruthlessly stratified than the one we live in now. Nor is it enough simply to eliminate all irrelevant discriminations of skin colour, sex, cultural background or family upbringing. We need full equality of material conditions – equality of incomes, in the broad sense – as the foundations of social life; full equality that is modified only by such extra rewards to effort and capacity as can be shown to be necessary for an efficient division of labour.

Past failures have driven some to apathy, others to belief in revolution, and still others to denial of the possibility or even desirability of an egalitarian social order. These are the roads to tyranny. The only other alternative, the one which has my allegiance, is this: that we, once again, take our traditions of citizenship and democracy seriously in their infinite richness and inspiration. They offer the basis for a new fraternity without which neither liberty nor equality is possible. They offer, also, the political and social vehicles of progress towards a newly-integrated society. Our experiences of industrial, nationalist and racial conflict continually demonstrate the need for new equalities to replace old class-restrictive liberties and status-crippled fraternities. We have still to provide a common experience of citizenship in childhood and old age, in work and play, and in health and sickness. We have still, in short, to develop a common culture to replace the divided cultures of class and status.

To do these things is no easy task. Stratification is stubbornly resistant to change. The attainment of a new and sound basis for social order requires political will of a strength we have hitherto lacked. No one can guarantee that either the challenge will be accepted, or the response forthcoming. But I would certainly claim that what I suggest we need is also socially and politically possible. Its elements are in our social traditions and on our political agenda. Adversity itself is now sufficient to give social response to political initiative. Democratic politics is, essentially, a system in which citizens actively mould the final decisions binding on all. It works only if liberty of thought and expression is ranked first among rights, and the active exercise of citizenship first among duties. Political action is inevitably carried on by imperfect people in public office. Hence the constant need for an alert and knowledgeable citizenry to protect itself against oppression and to prevent the public services from disintegrating into organisations which serve the private interests of public servants. Bold advances towards wider citizenship – in Scotland for the Scots, in the workplace for workers, in the school for parents, in the locality for the neighbour, and so on, could evoke popular support. Of course, there is also opposition. There are always those who place private interest above public welfare. Patient persuasion has to be our principal weapon: for persuasion is democracy in action. Only if it is given constant priority can we both guard our freedoms and override the resistance of vested interest. Only then, but certainly then, has democracy the right to enforce its will.

That, all too briefly, is my view of our best way into the future. We have neither a paradise lost, nor a paradise to be regained. Yet we can, if we will, take heart from Milton's portrayal of the departure of our primal ancestors from the Garden of Eden:

> Some natural tears they dropped, but wiped them soon;
> The world was all before them, where to choose
> Their place of rest, and Providence their guide:
> They hand in hand with wandering steps and slow,
> Through Eden took their solitary way.

Colin Blakemore

Mechanics of the Mind

Extract from 'Madness and Morality'

Sir Colin Blakemore (born 1944), is a British neuroscientist. Aged just thirty-two when his talks were broadcast, he remains the youngest ever Reith Lecturer. His lecture series explored different facets of human consciousness. In his final lecture, he considers mental illness and questions why society attempts to regulate the behaviour of its members and tries to order them into normal and abnormal.

Gustav Fechner was the founder of a new and objective approach to the measurement of mental events. He hoped that the kind of strict experiments that had beaten the forces of nature into the laws of physics could work for the human mind as well. Yet, despite the orderly, reductionist nature of his ideas, Fechner, in 1860, permitted himself an extraordinary speculation about personal consciousness. The brain is bilaterally symmetrical; it has two sides, which are virtually mirror images of each other. Nowhere is this clearer than in the cerebral hemispheres: there is a deep cleft between the two halves, which are linked by an enormous strap, containing millions of nerve fibres – the corpus callosum.

If consciousness is a property of the brain (which Fechner certainly believed), what would happen if the cerebral hemispheres were literally split apart completely? As the psychologist, William McDougall, reported in 1911, Fechner asserted 'that if a man's brain could be mechanically divided into two parts without arresting the life of the parts, the nervous activities of each part would be accompanied by its own stream of consciousness.' But McDougall was convinced that no mere split in the brain could divide the mind.

This hypothetical, inconceivable experiment of Fechner

and McDougall has actually been performed; and its results are, quite simply, some of the most fascinating produced during research on the brain. The rationale behind this unlikely story is that an epileptic seizure originating at a focus of damage on one side of the brain can spread to the other hemisphere through the nerve fibres of the corpus callosum. The attack then takes on the terrible proportions of a grand mal convulsion, involving the whole body.

Now, in California, in the 1950s, experiments with animals had demonstrated that cutting the corpus callosum did not interfere in a gross way with movement or any vital function. So a bold (some would say reckless) surgeon decided to split the corpus callosum in a few patients who had intractable epilepsy, in the hope that it would moderate their fits. It did – to an unexpected extent. Not only did the convulsions no longer involve both sides of the body, but they were reduced in frequency, too, though the reason for this therapeutic bonus is still unknown. But what of the other consequences of this unlikely invasion of the mind. Who was right, Fechner or McDougall?

Roger Sperry and his collaborators, at the California Institute of Technology, who had already done much of the preliminary work with animals, had the chance to examine these people whose brains had been split. At first, the patients seemed remarkably normal; indeed, that had always been the conclusion in previous studies of people who had suffered damage to the corpus callosum. However, careful and often ingenious psychological testing revealed a bizarre mental syndrome.

Sperry took advantage of the known fact that the connections to and from one hemisphere are mainly concerned with the opposite side of the body. If a split-brain patient is blindfolded, and some familiar object, like a comb or a coin, is put into one hand, he can use that same hand to retrieve the object from a collection of similar things by touch alone. But ask the other hand to do it and the result is pure guesswork. Imagine that the patient is looking fixedly at a point, and a picture of an object is flashed momentarily just to the left of that point (so that it is seen only by the right hemisphere, because of the distribution of nerve fibres from the eyes to the brain). Now, the patient can select the object portrayed by sight, or even by touch alone, when he uses his left hand, but not his right, to choose from an array of objects.

Each hemisphere, then, seems whole in itself, but with only half a body to serve it. In Sperry's words: 'Everything we have seen so far indicates that the surgery has left these people with two separate minds; that is, two separate spheres of consciousness. What is experienced in the right hemisphere seems to be entirely outside the realm of awareness of the left.' Judged by any simple criterion, like seeing, feeling, remembering or moving, there is not much to choose between the skills of the two hemispheres. To that extent, Fechner was correct. Indeed, Sperry's descriptions convey an eerie impression that the split-brain patient is no longer one person, but two: both hands do, indeed, have minds of their own.

But 'mind-left' and 'mind-right' are not equal in every respect. The biggest difference between them (or, at least, the most obvious) is that one hemisphere – the left in all of Sperry's patients – does the talking. Put an object in the right hand or flash a picture on the right of the visual field, and the patient, or rather his left hemisphere, can tell you what it is. But show it on the left side, so that only the right hemisphere knows about it, and the articulate left is lost for words. So the mind that makes its presence felt, because it can speak, is that of the so-called major hemisphere, usually the left. To that extent, McDougall was correct. The speechlessness of the right hemisphere has been seized upon by some as evidence that the consciousness of human beings cannot be truly divided. But such an argument seems to me quite specious – rather like saying that a brain-damaged patient who simply cannot speak, but can understand perfectly well, is not conscious and therefore is not human.

The minor, right hemisphere is not even totally illiterate: it can read. When the word 'comb' is flashed on the left of a screen, so that only the right hemisphere can see it, the patient cannot say what was written, but can reach with his left hand and select the correct object from a choice. If a picture of a steaming cup of coffee is shown to the right hemisphere, the left hand can point out, amongst an array of cards, the one with the word 'hot' written on it. So adjectives as well as nouns are understood by 'mind-right'. But all the time the left hemisphere, speaking through the mouth of the patient, has no idea what is going on. By all accounts, the right hemisphere is not very good with verbs, but it does have the vocabulary and the syntactical ability of a young child.

And what is more, in certain respects the subordinate right excels over the 'dominant' left. It is much better at any job that involves recognising patterns and shapes and, particularly, complicated solid objects. The right hemisphere can draw quite well with its left hand, but the left hemisphere even has problems in copying simple diagrams of houses and cubes – it is much more at home writing than drawing. Recognising faces, surely an immensely important part of human social behaviour, is also, apparently, a speciality of the so-called 'minor' hemisphere.

Fascinating though these observations on split-brain people are, I believe they have been misinterpreted in their relevance to the functions of the normal human brain. Protagonists of different factions have all nurtured the idea that you and I have virtually independent sides to our brains and therefore to our intellects. The dominant side, usually the left, talks, writes, does mathematics, and thinks in a logical, serial way; the minor right side recognises shapes and faces, appreciates music, puts on its owner's clothes and works in a global, intuitive fashion. The verbal, ordered culture of the

Western world, dominated by scientific and technological progress, is, we are told, managed by the left hemispheres of its populations; the mystical, artistic and religious cultures of the East must be driven by their right hemispheres.

There is a vocal movement that calls (presumably with its left hemisphere) for the liberation of its right. Some psychologists, but most vociferously Robert Ornstein, want a revolution in Western education with more emphasis on non-verbal skills and the special attributes of the minor hemisphere, which are supposed to rule the cultures of the East. I can't help feeling that some Oriental Robert Ornstein, contemplating the material progress that those attributes of the left hemisphere have given to the Western world, might make just the opposite recommendation.

In fact, Hugh Sykes Davies, the scholar of English, recently attacked the 'rightist' movement, and complained that verbal skills are degenerating, not dominating, in our society. All this fiery rhetoric seems to me to be based on a curious assumption that the two hemispheres of a normal man are as divided as those of Sperry's patients. Under exceptional circumstances, in unusual people, the separate characteristics of the two halves of the brain might come into conflict. The author, J. M. Barrie, creator of *Peter Pan*, was ambidextrous; he even wrote his plays with either hand, and his desk is worn smooth on both sides to prove it. He was sure that his two hands had different characters and that he was inhabited by two different people. But in most of us there is a constant traffic of information between the two hemispheres, a tying-together of separate experiences, a sharing of special talents.

What we should be striving to achieve for ourselves and our brains is not the pampering of one hemisphere to the neglect of the other (whether right or left) or their independent development, but the marriage and harmony of the two. It so happens that the special mental territories of the minor hemisphere – spatial perception, pictorial recognition and intuitive thought – are not easily amenable to conventional education, nor is it clear that they would benefit from years of formal instruction. Systems of education, especially higher education (and this applies to every culture), seem designed to develop and exploit the powers of the hemisphere that is dominant for speech, for those powers depend most on factual knowledge and prolonged training.

The ripening of cerebral dominance is one of the most important processes in the maturation of the brain. Unitary control of delicate motor skills, like speech and the fine movements of the dominant hand, requires the firm planting of the special apparatus for their control in one side of the brain. To ignore the special role and the particular educational needs of the dominant hemisphere, and to encourage the minor side to take charge may produce deleterious consequences in behaviour. It could cause problems as profound as the disorders of emotion and speech, especially stuttering, that are attributed to another cultural interference with cerebral dominance – the forced use of the right hand in naturally left-handed children. This form of social brain control was common in Europe and the United States, and was virtually mandatory in the Soviet Union until quite recently.

The debate about liberating the minor hemisphere is only a fashionable twist to an ancient and inextinguishable aspiration of human beings – to control his or her brain; or, more often, to control someone else's. The brain is the organ of behaviour, and the dream of every leader, whether a tyrannical despot or a benign prophet, is to regulate the behaviour of his people. There is a growing fear that a considerable fraction of brain research is aimed at making such control a reality.

It is true that animals will work ceaselessly to receive electrical stimulation through electrodes implanted in so-called 'pleasure centres' in their brains. The most effective areas lie in the hypothalamus (which is involved in the regulation of motivated behaviour, like eating, drinking and sex) and in the nearby limbic system (which is thought to control emotions such as rage, fear and joy). It is also true that electrical stimulation at certain sites, or local damage at others, can calm the fiercest beast or turn a placid animal into a savage killer. The physiologist, J. F. Fulton, wrote that a certain tiny injury to a monkey's brain 'yields an animal that is formidably ferocious . . . I finally had to decree that no one should ever examine (such a) monkey alone, for . . . they attack to kill, and they single out the examiner's neck as their initial objective.'

There is, naturally, widespread apprehension, nurtured by popular publications and not always discouraged by over-enthusiastic experimenters, that such techniques will soon be part and parcel of everyday life. Such fears are, in the main, quite unfounded: fortunately, the sheer paraphernalia of experimental brain manipulation, the implanted electrodes, the cables and electronics, the tedious surgical techniques, make that kind of brain control beyond the reach of any modern-day Alexander or Genghis Khan who wishes to motivate an army or subjugate the world at the push of a button. And in any case, are our brains not already more totally disciplined, our opinions more firmly moulded, and our minds more sharply directed by the political and social environment than by any electrode that could be put in our heads? The stentorian voices of the mass media are more universally powerful than the indiscriminate persuasions of any mind-altering drug.

More illuminating than pointing an accusing finger at the motives of brain research is to ask why society always has attempted to regulate and order the behaviour of its members. The answer might lie in a very basic biological need to identify – in order to identify with.

Group selection is a term used to describe the operation of evolutionary forces on closely knit and interbreeding groups of animals, not just individuals; it was recognised by Charles Darwin as an important factor in the emergence of social behaviour. By forming collaborative groups, largely based on family ties, animals can improve their chances of surviving as a group, and hence of propagating their common genes. Biologists even seek to explain the most cherished of human ethical principles – altruism, heroism and unselfishness – in terms of group selection of shared genetic material. J. B. S. Haldane once remarked that he was willing to lay down his life – for two brothers or eight cousins! Now, the preservation of common genes amongst a social group by such acts of cooperation and self-sacrifice would be greatly enhanced by an ability of the individual to recognise in others those similarities in appearance and behaviour that betray shared genes.

One of the major factors in the evolution of human society is the specialisation of the brain to recognise and classify. That power may have had its origin in the discrimination of genetic similarities and dissimilarities in other men. An animal, like man, that could actively direct its altruism and shape its behaviour ethics to protect its own genetically similar colleagues would have had an enormous advantage in group selection. The roots of social discrimination today, then, lie in the group discrimination of yesterday. The intolerance of difference has produced such social cancers as apartheid in South Africa, the caste structure of India and the endless warfare of Europe.

Many of the most precious elements in human social behaviour, such as formalised sexual bonding and family structure, rich communal ceremony, and the embracing of ethical principles within religious codes, can be viewed as deliberate cultural exaggerations of inherited components of behaviour that favour group selection. The desire to regulate behaviour, even to bring deviants back to the norm, may be a further cultural embellishment of the logic of group selection.

Nowhere is this more evident than in the field of mental disease, where the questions of social intolerance of difference and the danger of active brain control become most profound. The problem of illness of the mind is a challenge not only to medicine but also to society. Each year, one man in fourteen, one woman in seven, consult a doctor about some form of mental disease; every year, 600,000 people in Great Britain are referred to psychiatrists. Because the very symptoms of mental disease are defined as aberrations of behaviour, they bring the sufferer into conflict with the community in a way that no illness of any other organ can. Diseases of the mind are an insult to the behavioural order on which society rests. Most of all, they are usually disorders of emotion, a function that the human mind has so carefully concealed under its cognitive skin.

It is no coincidence that, in history, the same treatments have been meted out to the mentally sick as to those other offenders against the order of society – the criminal and the heretic. At best, they have had their demons cast out or merely been imprisoned; at worst they have been tortured to death.

Textbooks of psychiatry try to achieve the same as the codes of secular law or religious commandments; they all attempt to establish definitions and boundaries for normal behaviour. But just as the law adjusts to the nature of crime, just as heretics alter the religion that they offend, so cultural evolution has benefited from certain extremes of behaviour. Visionaries like Joan of Arc and William Blake, artists like Van Gogh and Edvard Munch, were, by conventional definition, mentally disturbed. The paradox of cultural evolution is that, as it gains from the contribution of those people who deviate significantly from the norm in intelligence or inventiveness, in artistry or in insight, it also builds up resistance to change, and distrust of extremes, by its emphasis on group identity.

The more revolutionary schools of psychiatry – for example, that of R. D. Laing – argue that the definition of sickness of the mind is a product of a fault in society itself. The anthropological extension of this viewpoint maintains that, since mental illness is culturally relative, those whom we call mad might be able to function usefully in societies that we call primitive. The delusions and hallucinations of the schizophrenic might be admired, and the mentally ill could fill important roles such as shaman, or witch-doctor. But recent, careful studies of Alaskan Eskimos and the Yoruba of rural Nigeria have cast doubt on the opinion that the 'illness' of mental disturbance is merely and entirely a label that is tied on socially unacceptable behaviour. Both of these peoples have special names for mental illness, *nuthkavihak* for the

Eskimo, *were* for the Yoruba, and neither ethnic group applies those terms to their shamans and healers. The shaman in a trance is described by an Eskimo as 'out of his mind', but not 'crazy'. There is little respect for those who are thought to be genuinely mad: they are shackled or sedated by the Yoruba healer, they are tied to posts or locked in barred igloos by the Eskimos.

But if mental illness is not a unique product of our way of life, its definition has been stretched to make use of the special powers that society has assumed for dealing with those that it defines as different. In their book, *A Question of Madness*, Zhores and Roy Medvedev give a moving and bitter account of the enforced incarceration of Zhores Medvedev, the eminent Russian scientist, in a mental hospital, because of his stubborn opposition to local party bureaucrats and his public pronouncements against the Soviet state. Under the frighteningly broad definition of 'creeping schizophrenia' that is employed by orthodox Russian psychiatry, Medvedev was declared to be suffering from paranoia because he showed 'poor adaptation to the social environment'. Medvedev himself was relatively fortunate; he spent only nineteen days in that 'political asylum' before the torrent of protest organised by his brother led to his release. But others are not so lucky; and the abuse of psychiatric definition continues.

Although we are right to be indignant about this flagrant affront to personal liberty in the USSR, we should not believe that our own approach to mental disease is without fault. A lack of sound theoretical knowledge makes even adequate diagnosis unlikely. In a recent survey, 200 children who had been diagnosed as autistic were subjected to a second opinion. Only 33 were diagnosed as autistic by the second examiner, 53 were said to be childhood schizophrenics, 51 retarded, 7 deaf, and so on.

Just as the criteria for diagnosis are not rigid, so the methods of treatment are largely empirical. The use of surgical damage to the brain in the treatment of the mentally ill is certainly the closest that we come to the horror of socially-applied control of the brain, and it illustrates both the inadequate restraints on the treatment of the mentally sick and the poor theoretical basis for that therapy.

In some cases, like the use of the split-brain technique for the treatment of epilepsy, the methods and consequences had been carefully worked out beforehand with experimental animals. But psychosurgery, the treatment of emotional disorders by operations on apparently healthy brain tissue, proceeds with a lack of experimental background that would be considered inadequate in all other areas of medicine.

The whole of psychosurgery had its origins in a research report delivered by C. Jacobsen and J. F. Fulton at a conference of neurologists in London in 1935. They had been training two chimpanzees to remember where a morsel of food was hidden. One of them, called Becky, was particularly temperamental and became extremely distressed when she failed at this task. She would fly into a tantrum and refuse to perform when the food was hidden from view. Fulton and Jacobsen performed surgical removal of part of the frontal lobes of the cerebral hemispheres and they reported that Becky no longer became disturbed during the experimental task.

A Portuguese neuropsychiatrist, Egas Moniz, rose after the talk and asked: 'If frontal lobe removal prevents the development of experimental neuroses in animals and eliminates frustration behaviour, why would it not be feasible to relieve anxiety states in man by surgical means?' Within the year, Moniz and the surgeon, Almeida Lima, had started to perform operations on the frontal lobes of deranged patients, and by 1950 some 20,000 people around the world, including prisoners and children, had been treated this way. And all of this stemmed from an almost anecdotal observation on a single, nervous chimpanzee.

Worst of all, the effectiveness of these operations was evaluated by the very surgeons who had invested their careers in psychosurgery: failure was not easy to accept. And with any treatment for the mentally ill, it is difficult to establish with certainty the success of the technique itself because of the fairly high rate of spontaneous remission from symptoms and the undoubted value of the extra attention that special patients receive, whatever their treatment. However, it became clear that the benefits of gross psychosurgical methods were often minimal and sometimes the consequences were disastrous. Moniz himself, who won the Nobel Prize in 1949, was shot in the spine by one of his own lobotomised patients.

But, once established, psychosurgery became self-sustaining. It is still widely practised. The techniques are more sophisticated and the surgical lesions much more discrete, but the lack of moral restraint and theoretical background is just as serious.

Significantly, some of the strongest criticism of psychosurgery comes from the behavioural scientists whose experiments are quoted as justification for the surgical methods. Destruction of the amygdala, a part of the limbic system, is used as a treatment for extreme aggression, although in animals damage to the amygdala sometimes increases aggressive behaviour. Aggressive patients have also been subjected to lesions of part of the hypothalamus, dangerously close to regions involved in the regulation of eating and drinking. The rationale behind this procedure is that a similar operation in cats can abolish the ferocious behaviour that results from an earlier injury to another limbic structure, the septum. But the septum is not even a clearly defined area in the human brain! Other parts of the hypothalamus are destroyed as treatments for obesity and even a symptom called 'latent homosexuality'.

That other widely used technique, electroconvulsive therapy, which undoubtedly brought some relief to people with severe depression, was, nevertheless, based on even more obtuse and spurious theoretical justification. The present-day use of convulsive therapy stems from a revival of the eighteenth-century opinion that maniacs were best treated by a very severe physical stress, and from the entirely erroneous view that epileptics are protected from schizophrenia by their natural convulsions.

Of course, medicine must work empirically until it has sound theoretical grounds for action. Sick people need to be treated. But in most fields of medicine, empirical art has been rationalised, modified or supplemented through experimentally-derived knowledge of how the body works. New methods of treatment have grown out of careful and thorough experimental work. In the management of many diseases of the brain, this is not yet the case. To that extent, some aspects of neurology and psychiatry are like mediaeval alchemy practised with twentieth-century tools.

It is true that the growing use of drugs in psychotherapy, which is also not without its critics, has dramatically reduced the number of long-term admissions to mental institutions. But, far more important, the intensive research on the action of therapeutic drugs, much of it demanded by law before they can be used, begins to offer hope of an explanation of the biochemical basis at least of schizophrenia.

There is, then, the promise that research on the brain will provide a genuine rationale for the treatment of mental disease. But much more than that, it will give a greater understanding of the nature of human beings. The study of the brain is one of the last frontiers of knowledge and of much more immediate importance than understanding the infinity of space or the mystery of the atom. For without a description of the brain, without an account of the forces that mould human behaviour, there can never be a truly objective new ethic based on the needs and rights of people. We need that new ethic if we are to overcome the intolerance of difference, which has entrenched society in dogma and discrimination – to dispel the naturalistic fallacy of arguing that the way we do behave is the way we must and ought to behave.

Revolution, social as well as scientific, grows out of knowledge. Only when the choices for action are transparent can proper choice be made. In the words of Mao Tse-Tung: 'We can learn what we did not know. We are not only good at destroying the old world; we are also good at building the new.'

I have described the brain as an organ, as a part of the body no more magical than the heart and the liver, which were themselves once thought to do the job of the brain. But also I have tried to show that the actions of the brain are quite unlike those of any other organ, because they determine the behaviour of one person towards others. The brain struggling to understand the brain is society trying to explain itself.

1972

Andrew Shonfield

$\sim$

Europe: Journey to an Unknown Destination

Extract from 'Melting Pot or Bag of Marbles?'

Sir Andrew Shonfield (1917–1981), was a British political economist and author of *Modern Capitalism*. His lecture series, delivered two months before the UK joined the EC (European Communities), debated the prospects of closer ties between Britain and Europe. In his first lecture, Shonfield explores integration between the European nations and questions the reasons for the European Community. He explores the power structures which create the Community's foundations and asks how joining the EC will affect Britain and all European nations.

At the climax of the great debate on British entry into the European Community, the argument sometimes sounded something like this. One side was saying that the whole operation was a disgraceful and unnecessary surrender of national power to conduct our own affairs: unnecessary because the European Community was essentially a feeble thing which would, if we only let it be, go away. And the other side, while urging us to brace ourselves for a great historic decision, told us authoritatively not to worry because the Community really had remarkably little power in practice to change the way in which its member states run their national affairs. Well, which is it? Feeble or powerful? Historic or a dead bore?

I must admit that there are occasions when I find myself oscillating between these two views. The feebleness of the organisation was very much in evidence during the bleak years of General de Gaulle's rule in the sixties, when the French government seemed bent on blocking any move that remotely threatened to give the Community a bit of extra authority. But even as late as 1972, under a very different French President, I was given a depressing demonstration of how this narrow view of what the Community is about continues to exercise its influence.

In January 1972, when Britain was about to sign the Treaty of Accession, I happened to be in Brussels, and found that a violent argument was in progress about the precise form which the legal document should take. In particular, was the current chairman of the Council of Ministers, M. Thorn of Luxembourg, to sign on behalf of the Council, which had agreed the terms with Britain, or not? One would have thought that there could have been no doubt that he should. But the French government representatives insisted that this had not, after all, been a 'Community exercise' but a negotiation between six governments, acting in their own individual capacities, which had simply agreed to accept a seventh into a club they had formed. It became evident that the French attached the very greatest importance to this metaphysical distinction between what the European nations do acting together and what they do as members of the European Community. They were still battling hard to keep the Community as such out of the business of signing the treaty when I left Brussels, forty-eight hours before Mr Heath and the prime ministers of the other candidate countries were due to arrive for the ceremony. They managed to settle it in time. But the event brought home to me the extent to which the detailed operation of the Community powers is today being jealously observed and controlled by the member governments. This is no European melting-pot. Indeed, most of the time it looks more like a bag of marbles.

However, I think one can show that in practice it has

rather more cohesive power than that. One has to look at individual cases: I shall start with a couple of recent decisions made by the European Court of Justice. They weren't exceptional decisions: I picked them out of the newspapers when they were reported in the course of a couple of weeks in the summer of 1972. In one of them a British company, ICI, was fined $50,000, and so were half a dozen other European chemical firms, because they had operated an agreement to fix the prices of certain chemical products at an artificially high level. The Community was collecting close to half a million dollars from some of the biggest firms in Europe and ICI was included, even though it is a British firm, because its trading activities in the six countries of the Community made it liable. The Community has that sort of power over people outside.

The second case concerned a tax imposed by the Italian government on the export of works of art. The court held that the Italian government had no right to exact such a tax on goods that were sold to other countries in the European Community, because it meant treating art-buyers there worse than Italian buyers. In consequence, all the money that it collected in this way from 1962 onwards is now to be disgorged by the Italian state. A final example, also in that same fortnight last summer: a question was raised in Brussels about the special tax reliefs and subsidies given by the British government to industry in development areas. Were these, in fact, higher than the level on which the Community members had agreed for themselves, and would the result be to give an unfair competitive advantage to certain British products that would ultimately be exported duty-free to the Common Market? Britain will probably be called upon, once it is a member of the Community, to prove that this is not so.

These three examples, taken almost at random, will serve as a means of exploring the kind of power which the Community has, and its limitations. One characteristic which is common to them is that the point of contention – the issue which leads the Community to lay down the law – derives from a prior agreement among the member states not to do certain things: not to rig prices, not to tax trade with another Community country, not to use subsidies for development areas to gain an unfair commercial advantage. In fact, the Community in its original form was largely built around the idea of a compact of abstention: governments agreed to get rid of all tariffs on trade among the member states, and then to abstain from interference with the free movement of goods, of persons and of money within their combined territory.

Now, agreeing on a number of specific things that governments will not do is much easier than arriving at a positive agreement on a line of action to be taken in common. It is plodding work; and the results, when they come, are very unexciting. If, for example, you want to make sure that all the beer-drinkers of the Community have a free and equal choice among the beers produced in the different member countries, and are not prevented from exercising this choice by local by-laws laying down special standards, then you first have to get an agreed definition of what is beer, and of its different varieties. It is surprising how many there are. Unexciting work – and a natural catchment area for music-hall jokes. It is extraordinary what intensity goes into these arguments about definitions of types of beer and suchlike – not to mention wines, which arouse even more violent, southern passions.

Then why bother with this kind of detail? Does it matter in the end? The answer to that is that these details, when added together, do affect a substantial segment of people's lives. And they are not the kind of details that can be left as loose ends: if the Community does not take responsibility for making a single common rule, then the individual governments will produce a number of rules of their own, some of which will conflict with each other.

Finally – and this is really the important point – the European system, as a piece of political machinery, depends on the constant testing of the collective will of the member countries to tackle any and every source of friction between them. When it comes to the big decisions, agreement often depends on a package deal involving a large number of apparently small matters, some of which happen to loom quite large in a particular nation's local politics. Wine is an outstanding example in France, beer in Belgium and Germany: you might lose an election on them if you got the answer wrong.

This, then, is at the back of the complaint which is so often heard, that the community is too 'technocratic'. The people who run it are technocrats, and they have got to be. More and more, as the Community has become engaged in the management of private power whose reach extends beyond the limits of the nation state, its technocratic character has been reinforced.

Why a Community?

The essential argument I am advancing is that the Western industrial nations are by now so intermeshed with one another at so many different levels that it grows increasingly difficult for a single national government on its own to exercise effective power over many of the actions of its citizens. In these circumstances it has a choice of three options. It could insist nonetheless on its exclusive national sovereignty and inflict highly unpopular restraints and controls on the people it governs; or it could opt out of exercising any kind of public power over these private interests; or it could form a community of nations, aiming to exercise such public power jointly.

But why a community – and why Europe? Surely a straightforward international agreement between governments would do just as well? The answer to that is: yes, in principle there is no reason why this new type of supranational power should not be exercised jointly by, say, France and Australia and the United States. But in practice big political decisions of this kind are not made in common unless a number of other, mainly historical circumstances are present too. Chief of these are that the political leaders of the nations concerned should be convinced that they have a wide range of everyday problems in common, with enough understanding and sympathy for each other's approaches to allow them to tackle them together and arrive at common solutions and secondly, that they are happy with the idea that their national desires and ambitions for as far ahead as they can see should be worked out jointly with these particular partners, who will collectively be in a majority.

Now these are portentous conditions. They mean, for example, that it was inconceivable that Britain would have entered into an effective partnership with Western Europe until it had first lost its empire and then become finally dis-abused of the idea of the Commonwealth as the fulcrum of an independent British policy. It also means that the Americans, with a quite different view both of the capacity and of the long-term role of their nation in the world, are not yet ready to contemplate the conscious sacrifice of independence that goes with membership of a community of the new European type – a group of nations aiming at the joint exercise of public power over a widening range of everyday activities that have hitherto been regarded as the exclusive preserve of the sover-eign national state.

In order to be willing to engage in this sort of exercise a nation must not be too large. It also needs to feel vulnerable. I think that the absence in Britain of this feeling of reduced size and increased vulnerability in the period immediately following the war, when the Europeans took their first steps towards integration, amply explains why the British were quite uninterested in joining in at that time.

The fact is that while the modern state has grown vastly more effective in looking after the welfare needs of its individual citizens, its ability to conduct independent national policies in the face of new pressures coming out of the international system has been much diminished. We see this in the way in which very large sums of money hurtle from one country to another as soon as a particular currency comes under suspicion. Governments are no longer able to carry on the struggle to preserve the international value of their money in the old style, when they may find, as Britain did during the sterling crisis in the summer of 1972, that more than a third of the national currency reserve has gone abroad in the course of normal dealings in the foreign exchange markets in under a week. In short, the dramatic improvement in communications, the greatly increased mobility of people and money, and also the huge concentrations of corporate power in the hands of international businesses, taken together, demand the establishment of a new dimension of international public power. At the same time there is a parallel movement, less obvious but beginning to be significant, among associations of private and professional persons – farmers, trade unionists, certain scientists, even specialist professional civil servants – who find that the natural links for much of what they wish to accomplish are with their professional colleagues abroad, rather than with their own national governments. The transnational lobbies that are thus created look for some international political counterpart.

Now I call this amalgam of private groups and agencies transcending national frontiers, together with the official political agencies that have been established in and around the European Community, 'supranational'. But I am not using the term in the simple, old-fashioned sense of standing above national governments. Bits and pieces of the national governments are themselves part of the system; so are some of the parliaments and the businesses and the professional organisations. If, to return to the simile I used earlier, this is more like a bag of marbles than a melting-pot, the marbles are soft on the surface and made of some sticky substance, like putty, which keeps them clinging together as they are pushed around and constantly make contact with one another inside the bag. It doesn't sound very attractive, I know. It certainly isn't very coherent. It is much less satisfactory to describe than the simple, old-style supranational form of European government which was the ideal of the founding fathers of the Community.

And that is one of the problems which afflicts the men who run the European institutions in Brussels. They still see themselves in some measure as the guardians of an imaginary Ark of the Covenant – the embodiment of the supranational ideal which inspired Robert Schuman to launch his original plan for a European Coal and Steel Community in 1950.

There were strong motives then for the outright surrender of bits of national power that had been cherished in the past. France was scared by the prospect of the revived industrial might of Germany, and the Germans, for their part, who were still under Allied occupation, were eager to seize the opportunity offered to work their passage back to international respectability. Encouraged by their first success with the Coal and Steel Community, the European federalists next tried to hustle the French government into a military agreement to amalgamate its national forces in a single European army. Pierre Mendes-France, who was French Prime Minister at the time, has never been forgiven by the federalists for the defeat of that proposal in the French Parliament. The rejection of the European Army in 1954 represents the decisive failure of their favourite post-war strategy. *La fuite en avant*, they called this strategy, which means roughly: 'headlong flight into an unknown future, in order to escape from a fearful present'. They of course believed that they knew what the future would really be – a fully federal Europe.

Traditionally, federations are made by wars – or, if not, as in the case of nineteenth-century Switzerland, by the fear of war-like neighbours. The Swiss cantons, in 1867, having had a nasty taste of Louis Napoleon on the one side and not relishing the prospect of facing Bismarck's new military power in Germany on the other, decided to surrender some of their cherished independent power to a central authority. In the Europe of the 1950s it was thought by some that the combined impact of the Cold War with Russia and of the need to create a rearmed Germany so soon after the end of the last war might have a similar effect. I suppose it was just possible that this might have happened, if Soviet Russia had been more openly aggressive and West Germany less orderly and manageable. But the opportunity for the 'flight into the future' quickly passed. And now we have to try to create a modern surrogate for a federation without the benefit of war or even a serious threat of war in Europe. It is a unique exercise, because it means that every step has to be conducted by agreement between states. There is no means of coercion other than moral pressure.

Common Social Aims

It was to this fact that I was trying to draw attention when I called this series of lectures 'Journey to an Unknown Destination'. Unlike the old-style European federalists, we don't know what the final answer will look like – or even should look like. But in any case it is not the point of arrival at a final union which it is important, or even possible, to foresee: it is the joint decision to embark on the enterprise, and the experiences along the route, that matter. We can, however, say something about the conditions that will have to be fulfilled if the venture is to have a reasonable chance of going forward. What is perhaps the most important of these conditions is not to be found anywhere in the basic Treaty of Rome or in other official documents of the Community. But it is implicit in what I might term the philosophy of building a community, which I set out earlier. The institutions of the community, on this view, are not instruments designed by a unique and irreversible act of will to carry out a clear-cut common purpose, but rather the expression of a set of common circumstances continuously shaping the societies of all the member nations. Now if one of the members were suddenly to decide to adopt a radically different set of social and political objectives, that would create enormous difficulties for the whole enterprise. The same would be true if the conditions of daily social life took on an entirely different form in one of these countries: for instance, if one of the national governments were faced with such strong opposition from its citizens that it could no longer enforce the law, except by the constant use of police violence.

It is obvious why in the latter case such a state would be a very poor partner in the building up of a community. For one thing, it could not give a reasonable assurance to its partners that the compromises and bargains with them which it made now would be fulfilled a year hence. The first rule, therefore, is that a community depends on having national governments which do in fact govern, and that the process of governing must be based on a large degree of continuity of public support. That means that a one-party state like Spain, quite apart from any other objections to it, would be an impossible partner. In any case, so much in the building of the Community depends on the spontaneous activities of independent interest-groups operating freely across national frontiers that dictatorships cannot be accommodated. On purely practical grounds, too, it would be vastly inconvenient, to put it no higher than that, if, in any dealings with the Spanish government, the others had constantly to be saying to themselves: 'And is this one of the bargains that will be kept when General Franco dies and is replaced by goodness knows whom?'

The other point – the need for the actual conditions of life and the social assumptions behind them to remain broadly in conformity among all the nine future members of the European Community – is a more complicated one. I am not saying that there is no room for differences in social policy. The Germans, for instance, have a much more generous old-age pension scheme, spend far more on it, than most of their partners. The British have invested more of their resources in the National Health Service. There is no reason why this should cause conflict. But consider what would happen if one of the countries moved sharply to the right and decided that the state should drastically reduce its financial responsibility for matters connected with the social welfare of its poor citizens. Say it adopted a reform to make everyone, including the poor, pay the going commercial rate of insurance for social security: since the poor are naturally high risks they would have to pay more than others, and this would result in greater social inequality. It would be very hard for the other nations, with their established policies of public responsibility for welfare, graduated income tax, pursuit of more equality, and so on, to agree on almost any common social or economic arrangement with the country in question. Inevitably, a number of subjects would arise – pensions, taxes, safety and health regulations – on which it would be necessary, but almost impossible, to collaborate. The Community could hardly manage to move forward with this country as a partner.

But now look at the matter from the other end of the political spectrum: not a reactionary right-wing government in pursuit of inequality, but an extreme left-wing one, aiming at a rapid and profound redistribution of wealth and income. Here the open frontiers of the Community, the agreements to abstain from impeding the movement of people, goods and money, would greatly complicate the political problem. The danger would be that, for example, an exceptionally heavy tax designed to discriminate sharply against company profits or the ownership of capital would induce the people who felt they were being badly treated to move their resources to other, more friendly parts of the Community. A single national government on its own would find it very hard to stand up against this.

There are other reasons why a major deviation in social and economic policy by one country, whether to the left or to the right, would be impeded by the complex of social and political forces which make up the European Community. I don't, of course, mean one of the familiar shifts of political power from main-line Conservatives to main-line Social Democrats, and vice versa. The Community has never found any problem with these. I am thinking more of cases like Castro's Cuba or the right-wing government in Greece. This perhaps explains why socialists of the extreme Left who insist on the revolutionary option have always tended to be instinctively hostile to the Community idea. The bizarre alliance of Michael Foot, a radical of the Left, and Enoch Powell, a radical of the Right, during the debates on British entry becomes more explicable on these grounds.

But how important is it in practice to the socialist Left to keep the revolutionary option open? If I may refer again to my central argument about the reasons for the emergence of the European Community, you will understand my doubts. For I see the Community essentially as the expression of a common fact of national life: the fact that the advanced industrial countries of Western Europe are today in an increasingly exposed and vulnerable position, and that they are less and less in charge of their individual national destinies. We live with more international constraints on our freedom of political action than many politicians care to recognise publicly. Giving up the revolutionary option by joining an international group which deliberately accepts these constraints will, in my view, be lamented chiefly for the loss of a favourite form of rhetoric rather than for any practical effect that it may have on the policies of the socialist parties of Western Europe.

1971

Richard Hoggart

Only Connect

Extract from 'A Common Ground'

Richard Hoggart (1918–2014), was a British sociologist and lecturer in English Literature. His expert testimony at the *Lady Chatterley's Lover* trial, arguing that it was an essentially moral work, is viewed to have been a decisive influence on the outcome allowing publication. His lecture series explored concepts of how we communicate. In his final lecture, he evaluates the role of passing information to each other and asks whether new technologies will bring us closer together.

There's a phrase, 'the quality of life', which embarrasses some and is carelessly used by others, but which can't really be done without. A culture will always produce a picture of the world and ask its people to accept and approve that picture and the values which stem from it. So to talk about the quality of a society's life is not, as some people seem to assume, to produce a slide-rule of externally verified, desirable values and measure the society against them. It is to look and listen, to ask what values are encouraged within a society, what discouraged, what the society allows as norms without a risk for the individual of rejection or breakdown, how the society's patterns of values are changing. When you are trying to understand the quality of a society's life you are listening to much more than words, than its manifest assertions. You are trying to interpret its attitudes to children, to death, to ambition, to the old, to the individual conscience, to foreigners, to the sick, to learning, to leisure, to the arts, to the search for truth, to privacy.

It would be pleasant to think that all the talk about communication today reflected and respected this diversity and richness, but it rarely does. 'Communications' is a catchword, a cult word. Obviously, our means of passing information of

one sort or another from one place to another virtually instantaneously, to hundreds of millions, has developed with almost
unbelievable speed and effectiveness in the last couple of
decades. So what then? Are we really more in touch? A great
many people, some out of overwhelming enthusiasm, some
out of naivety, some because they can tell a good bandwagon
when they see one, assure us that modern communications
will soon prove such interim doubts groundless. One may be
tempted to ask, 'Where is the knowledge we have lost in information?' but (they assure us) we will soon see technological
marvels which are just around the corner re-create what they
are likely to call 'significant contacts one with another' – or
words to that effect. There are always new ways of squaring
the circle just around the next technological corner.

Objectively, publicly, politically, the realities are harsh
and not to be wished away or even eroded by technological
advances in themselves. For example, on any considered view
of their possible contribution to the development of understanding, the mass media are misused or misunderstood
in most countries of the world. By politicians who, once in
power, channel the uses of the media to their own ends, or
would if they were able; by intellectuals who ignore or make
easy judgments on them and so more surely leave them to
the politicians or to commercial pressures. One looks over
a sad and virtually world-wide panorama of the media in
chains: in chains to the foolish and narrowing purposes of
selling (always foolish and narrowing in their effects on the

medium); in chains to the narrowing and stifling purposes of the national powers that be and their insistent, fixed picture of what their culture is and shall be. We are not at letter C in the alphabet of good uses for the large public media. Here, an art really is 'made tongue-tied by authority'.

Yet modern centralised mass societies are very anxious to 'get over', 'get across', to show that in spite of all the evidence they know and respect the human scale. The technological marvels chatter day and night all round the globe; the satellites circle the globe night and day; almost instantaneously millions from many nations can watch the same grand or amusing or terrible occasion. But to a great many people modern societies seem deaf: it seems harder and harder to reach any 'genuine, real, authentic . . . meeting, encounter, confrontation, dialogue'. I am using those popular words – they have become clichés too – deliberately, because their common qualities point plainly to what is felt to be missed: the sense of a meeting between human beings. Even the big exercises in communications, designed to alert us all – as individuals – to some public danger, to increase our awareness', too often look like substitutes for personally responsible action. Small wonder some people settle for unilateral opting-out. I think they are mistaken, but it's up to me to justify my position: in general, the evidence runs their way.

Direct old-style rudeness is less off-putting than those computer-programmed relationships which make you into an object, not a person: an object to be looked after maybe, but not known. Of course, we can't know all the people we are likely to meet in a lifetime nowadays; conventions for decent distancing are necessary. I do not object to those. I object to carefully calculated closings of the distance for the sake of a temporary imitation of contact. Still, cursing others won't get us far. We have to start with ourselves, with our own difficulties in saying what we mean, with finding a language fluent enough to express our individuality, vulnerability and wish for direct and honest contact.

We have to start at home, within our own society. If we can't get in touch there, there's not much hope further afield. But the balance – between home and away – is tricky. Over-immersion in one's own culture is far more common than internationalism without roots. Think of the many thousands of people who give so much of their attention to clubs or other organisations which are supposed to express some great national tradition – often military or monarchist. Sunday mornings in uniform. You meet them all over the world and, though their decorations differ, their expressions are alike. Could such national groups talk to each other? It's doubtful if they could swap anything except bits of medal ribbon.

To be culture-bound to this degree is to be stiff-necked. Most cultures have a good or at least a favourite national drink, curious ways of greeting when they drink, peasants with pithy down-to-earth sayings, rich stories of wise saws and rugged metaphors, heroes of wars won and lost, strange rituals with flags or the like on set days, and all the rest in the galleries of national cultural bed-warmers. To think these are grounds on which we are likely to appreciate cultures other than our own is to assume that, from the clash of cultural generalities or the swapping of old paraphernalia, precise comparative observation may come or effective connections be made. To be caught up in this hinders the appreciation of other cultures and of your own, and keeps you out of touch with whole areas of yourself.

There was an interesting contrast on one of the two government committees on which I have served, the one about broadcasting. A Welsh witness harangued us on the dangers to Welsh culture: something had to be done at once or the culture would be irretrievably lost. That there was this acute danger was chiefly the fault of the English and especially of the stuff they pumped into Wales via the mass media. The answer, we were told, was to let Wales have its own television channel, just as it already had a radio channel for extensive broadcasting in Welsh. The English would have to find the money. It would be dear, but little enough repayment for all the ills the Welsh had suffered at the hands of the English. Then a truly Welsh culture could be put down that channel for several hours a day. The new technological world would come to the aid of the old. All in all, it was a classical instance of cultural chauvinism – in this case, very aggressive – combined with the attempt to use modern mass media for predetermined external purposes. Later, in Scotland, a man from the Highlands said there was a lot he was bound to regret in the changes going on all around, but a lot he couldn't regret. He described how he tried to make the changes carry over with them some of the best in the old style of life, and ended: 'You can't put a ring fence round a culture.'

No culture has the whole truth or a truth so particular that it will be irreparably violated by contact with others. We can connect, we have to connect: not by hands-across-the-sea junketings or by the solemnities of most attempts at 'international understanding', but by a fully faced realisation of common qualities, the ribs of the universal human grammar. If we are to respond anything like fully to cultures not our own it helps to have known, known sensitively and intelligently, our own culture. Our own culture will be a prison unless we can surmount it and become in a certain sense cultureless, international. Yet internationalism is a shallow grave unless we know something about what roots are, and how strongly they affect us all our lives.

Room for action

When I started to prepare these lectures I knew roughly the area I was going to work in. I knew to some extent the kind of things I wanted to say. I didn't know how much I would find the argument altering as I went along, or what new things I would discover en route. I didn't know, until I found myself writing with special heat or at greater length or repeatedly about some parts of the argument, the shape and pressure of my own relations to the themes. I didn't know, for instance, how often important elements in the argument were felt inside me as paradoxes, and I have still not quite worked out what that means.

I didn't realise till quite late in the preparation of these lectures how much a couple of groups of very large assumptions lay under all I said, or how much I would come to recognise that those assumptions, so much taken for granted at home, seem strange in large areas even of what is called the 'developed' world.

I now realise more sharply how much I have simply taken for granted the primacy of the individual conscience, the belief that any wider commitment has to start from and satisfy that conviction. So the first group of assumptions can be clustered around a statement like this: the individual matters, and matters more than the society. It seems so simple to agree to, but when you look over the world you see how few assume it or, if they professedly believe it, will honour it – and the deniers and ignorers are often in power. Moving out from that core statement, we come upon related ideas: that the attempt at honest speech, first to yourself and to your nearest and dearest, matters and is the essential basis for honest speech on a wider front; that the commitment to truth matters and makes special pleading of all ideologies; that, though to reach the truth is difficult and we may never be finally 'objective', though our responses are always culture-affected and to some extent relativist, we are not in an absolute sense culture-bound: we can go a long way – by trying hard – towards stripping ourselves of hidden biases. That no single one of us can be quite objective does not justify imposing a single ideological position on all the individuals in any one society. Individual opinions are not aberrations or self-indulgences: they are the only foundation for collective positions which do not deny the fullness of human nature. I know that there still exist societies where traditionally the collectivity has counted for more than the individual. I am not talking about such societies. I am talking about the insistence in some large modern societies on obedience to the state as an entity and to its ideology. An ideology is less than a culture, and a state less than a community.

It follows that there is what feels like an absolute difference in kind, a difference a great many people are given little opportunity to recognise, between a 'disinterested' statement or analysis or exploration, made by a man free to go to the limits of his own strengths, weaknesses and courage, and all those other kinds of trimming which so greatly outnumber disinterested work: from low-level prejudiced proselytising to plainly doctored history, to middlebrow having-it-both-ways successions of fashions, to bland high-level intellectual acrobatics within the ring of a preset philosophy into which the shock of any other way of seeing reality is not allowed to penetrate. Then one realises that for most people all over the world virtually everything public that is offered, in print or over the air, is interested, meant to tickle their fancies or arouse their emotions or hammer at them for the sake of some other purpose – to get their money or their votes, to sell to them and go on selling, to keep them in line – not because the truth is great and should prevail. If you have been much used to 'disinterested' writing it is almost physically claustrophobic to read this stuff for any length of time. Reading the lower-level material is like passing your days in a waxworks show: all those set and painted imitations with no sense of depth, whether of character or in time. Reading the higher-level stuff, you feel terribly sad at the extent to which 'intellectuals' and 'artists' can be redefined or will redefine themselves so as to fit a particular national position.

At this point the sense of loss becomes so strong you are tempted to think the relativists are right, that all our talk of free men trying to describe themselves and their experiences as they find them, for their own better insight and that of those who may care to listen, is just an attractive delusion. If this is so, and since one wouldn't want to be the other kind of writer or artist, a calculator or servicer, the best course may be to have nothing to do with any profession in which we are expected to 'speak to each other' outside our own circle, but to get a job working with neutral materials – cleaning streets or tending forests – and confine our attempts to be in touch to our day-by-day, face-to-face, private and chosen and known circles. But that rather attractive despair would be premature. The roll-call of those who, even within systems which do not recognise their right to do so, have asserted, through art and politics and religion, the power and independence and courage of the human spirit trying to see life steadily and see it straight is too long, and the achievement itself too impressive, to justify backing out now.

This group of assumptions, I said earlier, contains the idea that men wish to reach what they insist on calling 'the truth'; wish to write not for the sake of 'our society' or 'our people' but because it matters to tell things as they are, to – in a lovely phrase – 'give things their proper names'; that men wish to reach others on that basis, not as a large block but as individuals who also respect the search for truth; that larger groupings are justified by the assent all the individuals within them have given to a value – the respect for truth – outside them or the larger group; that when a man says, 'Whatsoever is beautiful, whatsoever is of good report' he is talking about something he believes he can from time to time recognise and hopes he would continue to recognise even under pressure to deny it, something worth his love and loyalty, something bound up with his own sense of self-respect.

He may feel unable to say unequivocally, 'The truth is great and shall prevail,' but even if he were publicly to deny the truth under stress he hopes that in his heart of hearts he would still know that he had denied the truth. So these assumptions contain also the idea that a man should be free to try to live up to those ideals as a matter of his own choice, not hindered (if not helped) by powers outside; that he is free, it follows, to criticise the status quo if his sense of the truth leads him that way; that he has some room for action as an individual and as a member of groupings other than those arranged by, or smiled upon by, the authorities, room for action which seems to him right.

From there it is a short step to the idea that a healthy society should have within it many voices arguing in different ways, including especially voices arguing against the prevailing outlook; that a society ought to be able to stand such a strain direct rather than prohibit or employ elaborate cancelling-out and corralling devices so as to drain criticism and counter-arguments of their force. Societies, like people, have a natural skill at reducing and circumventing irritants; they have complicated ways, not all of them deliberately decided on by the authorities, of trying to ensure that 'free' speech is made futile, and sometimes it seems as though they have succeeded. But it is not so. In some places now and again – perhaps in most places from time to time – something gets through: the law defies the government, to give what seems the just judgment; the broadcasters defy the authorities and say what exactly did happen; and the press, against its own commercial interests, does the same; some teachers refuse to put out a line they know to be biased. Keeping up that pressure on all fronts is one of the best and hardest things we can put our hands to.

Fellow-Feeling

I am still teasing at the ramifications of those first assumptions and reach down now to an even more basic sense, one which underpins the wish itself to speak straight to one another. It is the idea – which I used never to think about but now find extraordinary, strange and compelling – of fellow-feeling: fellow-feeling based, not on the fact that we all belong to a particular national culture, nor on an abstract internationalist commitment, but on recognition of our common humanity, a recognition that we each rent the earth for only a short time, and that sorrows come to us all which we must bear as best we can.

Then one remembers Keats's quietly astonishing remark, 'Men, I think, should bear with one another'; or Yeats's old men looking out at the world, 'gaiety transfiguring all that dread'; or a less-known statement but of the same general kind, George Orwell's about the postcards of Donald McGill: the cards you can buy at the seaside, full of middle-aged wives with enormous bottoms, and little beery husbands leering at what used to be called flappers, and nagging mothers-in-law. After he had looked at the cards for a long time Orwell said: 'When it comes to the pinch, human beings are heroic.' One will go a long way with a man who can look at what seems shabby and unheroic material and produce a conclusion like that. Against such phrases I always find myself setting another: far from seeing men as brothers, it sees them as things to be manipulated. A cold, baleful eye looks through you, calculating the odds, and says: 'Stone dead hath no fellow.' The sense of fellow-feeling denies all abstracting hierarchies and rationalisations: it provides the basis for moving out beyond national cultures to make contact wherever someone else is willing and free to listen.

I remember, on first reading Dostoevsky, being impressed by a scene in which a father is humiliated before his small son. He is humiliated to the depths of his spirit at being so lowered in the eyes of one for whom he had been, naturally, a great man up to that moment. It is not a matter of the father's pride in himself, but of his love and concern for the boy. For me the scene marks one of those moments when the sense of common feeling bridges centuries and hundreds of miles and great differences between societies, a moment when one has a sudden and intense flood of sympathy because someone has looked directly and fully at his experience and shared it. I am not putting up a theory of intense moments in literature: I am using such moments as a way of pointing to one of the essential elements in full communication – the recognition of fellow-feeling. 'We are greatly more poetic than we know,' said Emerson: good literature starts from that belief.

Of my two main assumptions, the second is that we can in fact reach each other. These lectures have simply assumed we can, have started from that point as though it were an undeniable truth. It is not: it is a very large and, so far as I know, unproven assertion. It is possible, and to some people seems inescapable, to decide that in the end we do not communicate, and indeed do not really care or seek to communicate; that what we call our wish to communicate is only a saving – a face-saving – way of describing the wish to 'hear ourselves speak', to make others into mirrors of ourselves, to make them temporarily enter our private universes, so that we shall not feel so lonely, so that those private universes shall seem more valid. So that when we claim to have made contact with someone else we are only really saying that the echo-chamber has worked, that we have heard come back to ourselves the gratifying echoes of our own voices. The circle is complete, closed, vicious, not to be escaped from.

I have argued that communication starts with trying to speak more honestly to yourself, that it can then, if we wish, move out to trying to speak to others, and that it sometimes succeeds. But those are acts of faith. I find such phrases as 'now and for ever we are not alone' and 'we are members one of another' moving. Perhaps that's because of the beauty of the language. I want to call them 'right' and 'true', though, in their suggestion that our attempts to come together are not simply the defensive groupings of existential galley-slaves, or the huddling together of frightened kittens, but something more: a sign that we have a regard for the truth and a wish truthfully to discuss the nature of our common lives. For comfort, yes, but not for a cowardly or self-flattering comfort: rather, for the comfort of being better able to face through understanding the buffetings of experience. I believe all that, even though I cannot prove it. Which means I believe also that when we listen we do try to listen fully, are not all the time as we listen operating that elaborate selecting-machine which picks out for reception only those elements in what is being said that we are willing to take at any moment: those which suit our psychic books in one way or another, which flatter us or amuse us or at least do not disturb us. That process does go on, much of the time. But not always, not all the time.

But of all this too there is no proof, no proof that either side finally communicates anything accurately. Our whole world of discourse proves to be full of incredibly large assumptions of this kind. We are like water-boatmen: we assume a skin on the water of our common experience and then set out across it and hope to meet, because to assume otherwise would be to sink without trace.

What I've been calling my two main groups of assumptions – that it matters to communicate and that one can communicate – are inseparable or, better, they have a common source. They come together in yet another unprovable assumption – that experience is exchangeable, in what I called 'representativeness' in the second of these lectures, in the assumption that our personal experiences can have a more than personal meaning, can be shared, can be typical, symbolic, significant. My two main assumptions are joined in yet another way. If we felt in our heart of hearts that we were always doctoring our experiences, our attempts to reach others would all be at bottom forms of salesmanship, not attempts to tell things as we think they really are. The urge to communicate and the idea that experience is shared both rest on the belief that we can, at least sometimes, look at our experiences straight, and that it is important to tell people about them because other people count as we feel we count ourselves: in other words, this kind of effort at communication rests on a feeling – what I called a fellow-feeling – towards others which is intrinsically different from one which wishes only to use or manipulate them, or from an Ancient Mariner's grabbing them by the lapel so as to 'get something off his chest'.

I think, then, that an adequate approach to communications has to be founded on these main beliefs (they are, as I've said, unprovable, but we all believe more than we can prove): that the truth to experience against all preconceptions matters; that men matter to each other; that our experience pushes us out to find a common ground of feeling and of judgment; that our wish to tell and to listen is more than a disguised self-seeking or self-involvement, and that that shared wish is sometimes gratified.

Leon Bagrit

~

The Age of Automation

Extract from 'The Range of Application'

Sir Leon Bagrit (1902–1979), a refugee to Britain from Russia, was an industrialist and pioneer of automation. His lecture series explored how technological developments were changing the world. In his second lecture, he explores where advancements in computing could take us, predicting some twenty-first-century inventions.

It is essential for our future national prosperity in Britain that we should modernise this country, by spreading an understanding of the most advanced forms of technology as rapidly as we can and throughout the whole of our society. We must somehow induce industrial concerns to adopt these new techniques quickly and intelligently, and we must make sure that our universities, our technical colleges, and our schools are mobilised to produce the people with the background, the training, and the inclination which is necessary to bring this about. We must also see to it that the correct political decisions are taken to make it easier, not more difficult, to realise these aims.

A great many disciplines and techniques are necessary for the successful introduction of automation. A large plant would need to have a staff with an expert knowledge of, for example, operational research and linear programming. It would have to be closely involved in such highly specialised activities as information analysis, queueing theories, and other mathematical concepts. This need to recruit and encourage rather scarce and expensive experts may be one of the reasons why, so far, the amount of real automation in existence is very limited. I doubt if it is to be found at present in more than a hundred companies within the whole of Great Britain; perhaps the most notable of them is the Spencer steelworks.

But it is not necessary to believe that we are within sight of full automation throughout the whole of our industry in order to appreciate the enormous leap forward in productivity that automation makes possible. Nevertheless it would be a serious mistake, in my opinion, to think in terms of pre-automation and post-automation eras. In the real world, changes do not take place in such a neat and tidy manner. Conditions vary greatly from place to place and from industry to industry. The degree of automation which is economic is extremely elastic. Wages, transportation costs, markets – all these play a very important part in deciding to introduce more or less automation.

Automation is really an umbrella term for a complex of related systems. It includes, for instance, data processing and the scanning of information with alarm systems. It includes computation for specific purposes, for accountancy, for switching of information, for all kinds of recording, for observing, recording, and controlling every conceivable kind of activity – industrial, commercial, governmental, and social.

The heart of most systems of automation is an electronic computer. This is a very complicated piece of mechanism and of momentous importance, but it is, in fact, based on extremely simple principles.

Its distinguishing quality is a speed beyond human imagination, a speed measured in nanoseconds. A nanosecond can best be visualised as the time it takes for light to travel one foot – a thousandth of a millionth part of a second. Once we conceive that complex arithmetical sums can be done at that speed, we begin to realise the immense value of this new tool. It is a machine designed to read a binary code in which only two symbols are used – 0 and 1. All numbers can be made up of a combination of these two symbols, because, at a given moment of time, zero can be represented by there being no electrical charge, and one by a charge being present. We can detect and count the pulses passing a given point in the machine, and this allows us to accumulate information at very high speeds, in a form in which it can be read, transcribed, and used for calculations. Because of the high speed, we can afford to go through a large number of elementary and simple steps to arrive at a most complicated answer.

The means of retaining the answers we get, in what we call the computer's 'memories', has now reached a point where we can accumulate information, extract whatever we require, integrate with other information, make calculations using both existing and new information, feed the answer back into store, where it can be kept until it is wanted again, and compare it with further information as and when this arises.

Miniature Computers

A great deal of the future of electronic computers lies in the reduction in size, in the miniaturisation. Much of this has already taken place. We can now visualise, as a practical proposition, a computer, which has hitherto needed a large room to contain it, being reduced to the size of a packet of a hundred cigarettes. The significance of this is not merely that the size is smaller, but that the speed is increased in an unprecedented fashion, because the electrical pulses have shorter distances to travel. A higher speed in computers means that their complexity can increase very rapidly, too, and that they can more easily engage in activities in what we call 'real-time'. That is to say, they can calculate at the actual speed of the events taking place.

These machines can be made to do many things intelligently and can do them better than human beings, but they themselves cannot think. Any idea of 'thinking machines' is nonsense. They can be taught to improve their own performance by examining what they have done. That is true. But I do not think that we should call this thinking, although we can certainly produce machines which will learn more and more successfully from their own experience and so keep on improving their future performance as time goes on. They can accumulate information and sort out their own reasons for success and failure.

But to compare such machines to human beings is to endow them with intuitive qualities and with values and with subconscious sources of information, and these specifically human attributes they simply do not possess. Automated machines are only an extension of man's own capacities and not a substitute for man himself.

Nevertheless, machines like this can be used to do intelligent work if they are controlled by intelligent human beings, who exploit the machines by programming them to perform particular jobs really well. They can even be made to write their own programmes. But without the initial human master programmer they cannot even begin.

Not Thinking Machines

A great deal of nonsense about computers is talked by otherwise intelligent scientists and much confusion has arisen because of the need to use terms like thinking and deciding in describing what these man-designed and man-made machines do. But it is important to bear in mind that, in fact, they do not think or decide. They simply operate on the basis of a value which is put into the machine by the programmer. They can say what and when and how much, but unless initially the programmer gives them detailed instructions, they cannot operate at all.

One of the most terrifying uses of computers is for war games, the idea being that the military can safely and sensibly use computers to play at nuclear war. This is a substitute for the old game of playing at war on maps. If you lay down formal criteria for a win then, of course, this is a fair game, but no one knows what constitutes a win in a nuclear war, or if today a win for either side is even possible. Anyone who is foolish enough to believe that he has conquered the secrets of winning a nuclear war, because he has discovered the tricks of winning a battle on a computer, is a most dangerous man.

This is merely one of the threats and perversions that arise through the abuse and misunderstanding of the use of computers.

When, on the other hand, we aim at using computers for sensible and constructive purposes, it is evident that automation technology has completely transformed the means of collecting data, measuring it and processing it for all kinds of investigation and activity: but to exploit these possibilities new disciplines and new methods of organisation are required. These are now being developed and taught and standard practices are evolving from them. Today, for instance, no manager, book-keeper, administrator, or accountant can hope to remain aloof from the technological changes which are taking place around him.

Technology has invaded their realms, and although they may dislike and fear this, they must, from now on, work out their procedures in terms of the new sophisticated equipment and techniques which are being developed continuously. Although there is a growing awareness of this, there still exists a vast area where the possibilities are barely understood, let alone explored.

What can be measured can be controlled

It was Lord Kelvin who produced the terse and accurate comment on scientific endeavour that what can be measured can be understood. This has its modern counterpart – which is almost the motto for the Age of Automation – that what can be measured and made quantitative can be more precisely controlled. Man is not very well adapted for sensing or measuring accurately or frequently, especially where more than one or two variables are involved. Both manual and clerical tasks are accordingly broken down in order to fit the human capacity to observe, scrutinise, and control.

The need for man to be a part of a machine-system, in order to measure and control a situation, has hitherto proved a considerable barrier to progress. Automated machines, on the other hand, are not subject to these limitations, and consequently schemes for organisation and control can now be conceived in terms of the end-product, rather than of a number of intermediate goals. And these machines are not limited to fixed and predetermined control strategies. Their control action is being continuously modified, as new information is received; they are always adapting to fresh situations. New man–machine partnerships can now be worked out in the control of processes and operations which up to now have relied almost exclusively on unaided man himself as the control agent. This is on the way to being achieved in such different fields as air traffic control, clinical medicine, baking, and oil and chemical processing. In each case, careful preparation and operational research are essential to achieve a fruitful man–machine relationship, so that the machine is given only those parts of the task which it can do best and the integrity and importance of final human judgment and decision are preserved.

Yet we are only on the threshold of these momentous possibilities. But the new framework of ideas evolving round automation technology is going to demand a great deal of rethinking of established management methods. We shall need many more people trained in operational research and cybernetics, and there will have to be an awareness of at least the basic principles of these subjects by an even broader section of the community. From now on, no institution where private or public capital is employed on any scale will be immune from technological change, and what has begun to overtake business practice in recent years is already beginning to enter such less likely areas as hospitals and farming. Machines can perform any form of calculation, any type of book-keeping or accounting procedures. It is merely a matter of arranging the tasks to suit the machine. Machines can also carry out sequences of production operations, integrated by inter-process handling equipment.

Even by themselves, the three areas I mention – calculation, management accounting, and mechanisation, comprise a great deal of the industrial, scientific, and commercial activity of our society. Yet they by no means exhaust the ways in which automation can help. The food industry provides many interesting examples. The manufacture of ice cream, for instance, is now controlled by automatic method throughout, from the supply and blending of the ingredients to the final freezing, and baking is beginning to move in the same direction. This is surely overdue: it is surprising, even to the layman, to find how little instrumentation there still is in most continuous and expensive baking ovens. The bakery relies for the operation of its heavy investments on an experienced oven-man, and he in his turn relies on a great deal of what one can best call skilful guesswork in bringing the oven to the right temperature for baking. His skill lies mainly in allowing for variables in the process and for weather conditions. With long experience and a sound instinct he often guesses remarkably well, but by measuring automatically temperature, gas flow, humidity, and heat radiation levels it should be possible to specify exactly the conditions to be maintained for a particular type and quality of bake. In this way, we could design an automatically controlled oven of great versatility that could be switched from one product to another, maintaining in each case a constant and appropriate baking environment. This would allow the planned production of more uniform products with a saving of fuel and reduction of wastage.

A similar type of approach is applicable to a vast number of industrial processes, from brick-making to laundry-work, and from steel to cheese, to an extent that goes far beyond the capacity of man alone. And the problems to be faced in the future are going to demand even further extensions of man's sensing and controlling capabilities. The operations of widely separated factories, for instance, can be coordinated and controlled by automation systems, just as in a modern steelworks a complex of unit processes can be made fully interdependent.

Automation is not confined to commerce and the manufacturing industries. In the case of medicine, the wisest and most experienced specialist will inevitably have less knowledge of a particular condition than the medical profession as a whole; to arrive at his diagnosis in the classical manner, a doctor has to review what he knows and weigh it against the probabilities as he sees them. In the not too distant future, we can imagine him referring the symptoms to an electronic library. This will supply him rapidly with a list of diseases, and their characteristics, which are compatible with the symptoms. A medical automation experimental unit has already been set up at University College Hospital in London. Automation specialists and medical specialists are working together to develop methods of speeding up administration, diagnosis and research. The computer in use by the unit can search and tabulate medical record libraries, carry out statistical analysis, and help plan radiation treatment.

In medicine, as in other fields, human judgment, however, must still remain the final arbiter. The instinct, skill and experience of an outstanding man will still be invaluable in arriving at a correct answer, but the chances of an important possibility being overlooked will be much reduced. The usefulness of the computer could be extended to cover not only symptoms and diseases but also tests, allergies and treatments. The information would be checked continuously by the mass of clinical experience fed into it. In the case of research into, say, cancer, there would be methods of correlating lines of investigation and their results throughout the world. This would provide ready access to data to which neither the practising doctor nor the individual research worker could possibly gain access without machine assistance.

Hospital services could also benefit. A fresh approach, built around the framework of automation of data related to patients could deal with admissions, treatments, pharmacology, dietetics, clinical laboratories, wards, administration and research departments, each of which uses some part of the patient's data. Doctors' and nurses' time could be saved by using automation technology to collect, record, edit and transmit the appropriate data between the various departments of hospitals. This requires the rethinking of hospital methods and procedures in order to delegate to machines the things they can do best, and in this way to help solve the labour shortages in hospitals. Technology has a valuable part to play in increasing the efficiency of our Health Service and in giving us a more adequate return on the huge capital invested in it.

I hope it is clear, from the examples I have given, that automation is not merely a matter of 'hardware', of machines.

In none of the cases I have mentioned could one simply buy an electronic computer and use it effectively. The successful application of automation demands a combination of the right equipment for the purpose – that is to say, hardware – and adequate thought and intelligence – software. A computer system can be disastrous if the firm or institution which has invested in it lacks the outlook and the understanding to handle it.

A whole range of new possibilities is being opened up by the development of extremely small computers, using micro-circuitry developed for communication systems in confined spaces, such as in aircraft or missiles. The enormous reduction in size that has taken place during recent years can be illustrated, perhaps, by saying that, whereas the computer of 1950 needed a large room to contain it, the 1964 model is down to the dimensions of a suitcase, and by 1974 the normal computer will be no bigger than a packet of a hundred cigarettes.

In civilian life this kind of computer clearly has great advantages. It is now possible to envisage personal computers small enough to be taken round in one's car, or even in one's pocket. They could be plugged into a national computer grid, to provide individual enquirers with almost unlimited information. The availability of very small general-purpose computers is changing radically what we might perhaps describe as our computer philosophy. We can see that it is now possible to build computers with something approaching the amazing flexibility of the human brain. The human brain has a capacity which vastly exceeds the requirements of any particular moment. Today most computers are so large and expensive that they are generally confined to places and situations where their capacity can be fully used. But in the course of the next few years new techniques will enable computers to be produced so small and so cheaply that they could be carried about with no more difficulty than transistor radios. This will permit computers to be used in what, today, would be called a grossly inefficient manner.

This is one of the premises on which the American project, Project Mac, is based. The United States is now spending £5,000,000 a year on the development of a general-purpose computer which will be so easy to programme and to communicate with, that its services could be made widely available as a kind of public utility. The aim of Project Mac is to work out time-sharing techniques to enable a vast number of people to use a single computer simultaneously; to write master programmes that will allow people to do their own sub-programming, and to communicate with the computer in simple English. They are also aiming at developing a library of programmes of general usefulness. Any one of these would be immediately available through its code name.

Perhaps the most far-reaching use of the new generation of computers will be in the retention and communication of information of all sorts within national, possibly world-wide, information systems. This will enable decisions to be taken by people at all levels on a much more informed basis. Weather conditions and weather forecasts may be held in the system to provide local computers with the information for controlling both domestic and industrial heating and cooling plant. Complete air and road traffic situations may be stored in such a way that computers within the vehicle may be instructed to control the car or the helicopter safely to its destination. Car drivers could be told immediately about traffic hold-ups and road works and given alternative routes where delays were likely to occur on the direct road.

Everyone could be given access to a national economic computer. In this could be stored a vast amount of up-to-date details which could allow the individual worker, or a firm, to obtain the facts necessary for solving a particular problem. I am imagining, for instance, that one might want to know what the world output of certain commodities or raw materials was running at, or what the current rate of transportation loading was. A large number of commercial decisions are made every day, and it takes a long time before the result of all these interim decisions can be expressed in terms of profitability or Stock Exchange prices. By means of a personal computer service of the kind I have been describing, we could have a system whereby a business man would decide on informed economic grounds what action to take. There would probably have to be some statutory provision to compel him to feed his decision back into the computer to prevent it from being starved of facts. If this were done, the machine would constantly be primed with the latest information, not necessarily about each individual action but certainly about the cumulative effect of a large number of individual actions.

On the other hand, in many industrial and commercial applications we are moving steadily away from large, centralised computers towards much simpler decentralised units, systems of small, cheap, special-purpose units, rather like building bricks. These allow an engineer, familiar with his own industry and its technology, progressively to build up anything from a simple process controller to a system for the full automation of a complete works. By following this method we are able to turn away from the monster, expensive, all-embracing computer installation to a system of progressive automation. A start can be made with a very modest capital outlay, in the knowledge that any extension of the system is easily achieved on the firm basis of later experience. This new modular, building-brick, hierarchical system, known as Arch, provides maximum security in operation and allows individual managers to keep a personal interest in the processes under their control and, even more important, in the staff who are responsible to them.

Another possible development, which may sound a little fantastic at the moment, is the complete translating machine. We have already at our disposal means of converting human vocal sounds into numerical symbols. We also have some knowledge of how to convert numerical symbols into vocal sounds, so the time is not far away when the computer will be able to recognise the pattern of speech and to reproduce artificially a human voice. Once this stage is reached we shall be able to speak into a computer and get the sound translated into electronic symbols. These symbols would not necessarily repeat the sound in English. They could repeat it in any other foreign language with which the sounds could be made compatible. So that it is quite reasonable to conceive a personal miniaturised translating machine which you would carry in your pocket and which would allow you to talk to a Chinese in English and allow him to reply in Chinese. But you would hear his reply in English. There would be limitations no doubt for a long time to come in the kind of vocabulary available and its size, and there would probably be technical hitches of various kinds, until perfection was ultimately reached. We know the jokes like 'out-of-sight, out-of-mind' appearing as 'invisible idiot'. But technically there is no apparent reason why such an interpreting machine should not in fact be constructed fairly soon, if we are prepared to spend enough money. This proviso applies to all developments within the field of automation: finance for research is never unlimited, and any government or commercial concern naturally gives priority to those projects which appear likely to produce the most directly profitable results in the shortest time. And the order of priorities may well differ considerably from one country to another.

1954

Oliver Franks

Britain and the Tide of World Affairs

Extract from 'The Will to Greatness'

Lord Oliver Franks (1905–1992), was an English philosopher who has been described as 'one of the founders of the post-war world'. He served as British Ambassador to the USA from 1948 to 1952 and co-founded NATO. His Reith Lecture series considered what the future might hold for Britain and its platform on the world stage. In his final lecture, he asks how 'the nation' can be more effective politically, socially and economically, and argues that the responsibility of freedom must never be forgotten.

We have to make a choice in the next ten, perhaps in the next fifteen, years. We can live half in a dream and behave as if the world had not changed greatly or our position in it. We can live as if we need not bestir ourselves; as if the British Commonwealth was sure to go on of its own accord; as if it did not matter whether we get the Americans wrong or they misunderstand us; as if Europe was still the Europe we used to know; as if we could ignore the direct connection between the effort we make at home, our flexibility and efficiency in production, and our prospects in the world. Or we can live wide-awake to the changes round us and take our opportunity. We can be leaders and have a position out of all proportion to our population or our physical resources. We can make a real contribution to settling the great problems of the world.

I have left out on purpose: the division between the communist bloc and the rest of us, the new nationalism of Asia, the steady increase of armaments, and atomic and hydrogen bombs. I am sure we can brood too much on the Iron Curtain and the metaphysics of coexistence; and the possibilities of a third world war and mass destruction. We can be so fascinated by the dangers we contemplate that we lose the power to act. Sudden and uncontrollable catastrophe is possible, but it is no good looking at the future simply in terms of that hypothesis. The probability is that these problems and dangers are all long-term. We are going to go on living with them. There are no quick answers. I think it is obvious that we have a contribution to make. We have a sense of history. We know how to combine resolution in purpose with moderation in action. We are accustomed to making time an ally, but not an excuse. We might make the difference between peace and war.

The Choice before Us

We therefore face a moral issue. By our choice we shall declare what sort of people we are. My reading of history is that the British people have always been prepared to undertake and carry through what they believed necessary for the continuing greatness of their country. They have shown this in time of war and they have shown it again in these years of troubled peace. But their readiness always depends on a condition. It is this. They must see clearly and be convinced that what is said to be necessary really is so. How are we to reach conviction and stop being in danger of gently deceiving ourselves, pretending that we do not really face such a choice, or hoping that what we should like will happen anyhow, without our having to bother?

I said that the choice we make will show what sort of people we are. I had something precise in mind. In this half-century we have been forced to see that we cannot take civilisation, or freedom, for granted. A free society is a great achievement. But it is also a difficult thing, and fragile. To keep it, you have to work away at it all the time. Our kind of free society is a total democracy. By our choice we shall show whether we can carry its responsibilities or whether it is going to be too difficult for us. Here we confront yet another of our problems, the change we have made in ourselves. For total democracy is a new thing. In the United Kingdom it is the child of the twentieth century. To my mind it is still in the experimental stage.

Total democracy is democracy carried to its limit. In the United Kingdom it means that all men and women of twenty-one years of age and over have the vote. It has been natural, and perhaps inevitable, that the first effect of all having the vote has been to focus interest on the distribution of wealth. It has increasingly become the centre of controversy between the political parties. It has led to nonsense about the problems of production being solved while those of distribution were still to be worked out. The general effect has been to empha-sise political division. And this has been further stressed by the power of the great party machines developed to get the mass vote out, the narrow margins of victory at general elec-tions, the importance attached to party loyalty.

This emphasis is a weakness, for our kind of political democracy depends as much on the recognition of unity as on the fact of division. The recognition of a common responsibility for the interests of the whole community, the acknowledgement that there are national issues which should be debated and settled outside of party, the self-discipline in controversy entailed by these beliefs – these maintain the unity of a free society which alone makes party disputes healthy and constructive. They are our safeguard against civil strife, against the emergence of force as the arbiter of disputes.

I feel sure that if I were regularly present when the House of Commons is sitting, I should often feel that the quality of the debate was near that of a Council of State, with party advantage forgotten for the moment. But I am not – like nearly all of us. From the outside I catch more easily and more regularly the echo of disciplined feet marching into the lobbies, division after division. On the great questions of national importance which are outside party, we, the mass electorate, do not hear enough from our leaders. We need to be better informed, on foreign affairs, on economic matters, about what falls within our common responsibility for the general interest. How else can we give that measure of intelligent support to the government without which democracy grows weak?

There is a risk of too wide a gap developing between those who govern us and us who are governed. The gap grows naturally: it is closing it which takes thought and effort. We have to spend most of our time looking after our own affairs and taking an interest in the churches, groups, or clubs to which we belong. It is not easy to rise suddenly to a national point of view and look at the problems of Britain, overseas and at home, as responsible citizens. But those who govern us spend their working days on these problems. Their job is to take account of the changed world in which we live. They are accustomed to the complexities of our relations with our friends. Their outlook, their approach to the problems, the methods they use differ from our habits of thought.

It is at this point that some people take refuge in the notion of strong leadership. I should be the last to deny the need for the government to lead or its duty to do so. But the mystique of leadership does not fit in with our kind of democracy. Nothing can take the responsibilities of the citizens from them. Surely in Britain leadership is a complex and delicate art, and successful leadership depends as much on the enlightened support of the led as on the inspiration of the leader. If, therefore, we are to narrow the gap between those who govern us and ourselves, we shall need help from our leaders and we shall also have to help ourselves. But as we succeed and prove we can carry our responsibilities, we shall at the same time see more clearly and, I believe, choose rightly about the future of Britain. The moral issue with which I began and the operation of total democracy come together. Our governments will be able to carry through the broad policies we must adopt only if we understand and support them.

Response of the Many

I shall be told that this is not realistic. If seeing clearly and choosing rightly about the broad future of Britain is to be the function of the general body of voters, then it will never happen. It implies an idealised, a perfectionist view of human nature. And if you expect too much from human beings, you end by getting nothing. It is no good making everything depend on the response of the many. I disagree. And this is the heart of the matter. Our political tradition is built on the ability and willingness of the voting citizen to be interested in the general question of the community and take some individual responsibility for their solution. We presuppose a sufficient degree of unity and common purpose to be able to settle our affairs in debate. We have faith in reason as the chief weapon of democracy, not believing for one moment that we are purely rational beings but holding that reason can regulate our other activities and prevent a resort to force.

These are built-in presuppositions of British society. They were at work in the decision to make education universal in 1870. They helped to lay the foundations of a general secondary education in 1902. We were sure that the spark of reason was alive in everyone and could be brought out and developed. Total democracy is the test of our political faith. It is far harder to get understanding of the broad problems of the nation widely spread through the mass electorate than it was with the minority electorates of the last century. True, but this is the only direction of advance. It is implied by all we have done. After all, the price of keeping our free society is more than eternal vigilance: it is going on working at it.

I want to illustrate the sort of thing we can do. There are fields where I think we must first be helped by our rulers: there are others where we can do a good deal to help ourselves. As an example of the first, I take foreign affairs, both political and economic. We should gain a good deal if our leaders were rather less cautious in approaching the whole body of citizens, if they were more experimentally minded. This is the age of radio and television. And the old tag is true: seeing is believing. The power of television is great and will be used. They could put it to good use. What I observed in the United States makes me sure of this, as it also impressed on me the importance of mastering these new techniques of mass communication with the citizens in their homes.

Making the Nations More Effective

If our leaders would stimulate general discussion in the nation more often, outside the lines of party, on some of the broad attitudes we should adopt to the changed world, the nation would be more effective. And later, when they came to particular decisions, they would enjoy stronger and more understanding support and run less risk that sudden popular emotion would frustrate their efforts. Experiments like this would not infringe on the rights and privileges of parliament. What the citizen needs is to be helped to think out the general background of policy, the long-term assessments of the situation which lie behind the actual conduct of affairs.

There are difficulties. One springs from the progress of general education in Britain over the last eighty years. For education both builds and destroys. It is destructive of established authority and traditional opinion. The authority it recognises and respects is that of experience, of the man on the job, the man with active responsibility. These have the right to be heard and believed. In our political system Ministers of the Crown and their advisers, members of the Foreign and the Civil Service, alone in their different ways have the authority of direct experience. They are the people who are on the job.

The Ministers of the Crown most closely concerned with these matters in any government are the Foreign Secretary and the Chancellor of the Exchequer. I have worked with more than one Foreign Secretary and more than one Chancellor of the Exchequer. I know how hard driven they are. There is little time or energy to spare after the proper demands of parliament, of their departments, and of conferences overseas. They can hardly add to their duties. The question – and it is a big question – is whether the priorities are right. I am suggesting the case for revision.

Then there are Foreign Servants and Civil Servants. It

is our pride that the public service is outside party politics and serves whichever party is in power. But members of the Foreign Service, when posted abroad, frequently find themselves making speeches and leading discussions on foreign affairs. And at home I have noticed in recent years that senior members of the Civil Service have had rather more freedom to talk in public on the background of their work. I suggest that, if a wider knowledge of the background and general direction of foreign policy is urgently required among us all, there is room for a variety of experiments in closing the gap between us and them. This need not conflict with any essential principle. For myself, I am more worried by the risks of trying to guide twentieth-century democracy by nineteenth-century methods.

I was interested, when in the United States, to watch an experiment the State Department was making. In 1951, for instance, officials of the Department went out into the forty-eight States of the Union and made nearly 2,500 speeches. Meetings were held in the State Department, at the rate of one a week, to explain to various groups and organisations the broad aims of American policy. Beyond that, there were regional conferences at which the heads of national organisations discussed foreign policy with members of the Department. I know that one can never successfully transplant an American practice into the British scene, any more than one can do the reverse. But the problems of the mass electorate face the Americans in their continent as they face us in our islands. We can afford to view such experiments with indifference only when we know we have better answers ourselves.

My second example comes from the field of economic affairs. Our governments since the war have repeatedly appealed to us for restraint about wages and wisdom in the use of profits. I must admit that for a time I thought this advice sensible rather than profound. But now I believe the point to be of a different order. Our governments, it seems to me, have become aware of a new working principle in our democracy. They have insisted on it because, unless we see it too and act accordingly, our free society is endangered. But to think through and apply a new working principle in the life of the community is a major matter. It continues to be the business of us all because it is a question of our general attitude to life and work.

Let me explain what I am driving at. You know how the political parties are agreed that the state should aim at maintaining a high and stable level of employment. You know, too, that experience since the war suggests this aim can be achieved. High employment and the steady growth of production have enabled us to make great advances. These advances have brought other things with them. Almost anyone can find work. Profits are good, because demand is kept high enough to absorb what is produced. Again, labour shortage and good profits together reduce resistance to wage increases.

Wage increases which come from greater efficiency of

production are very good things. But when they do not, and the increase is passed on in higher prices, it does little good to those who get more and harm to those who do not. What is more, if this happens regularly, it whittles away the value of money. And if inflation gets out of hand, the danger is great. The line of argument is familiar, but the dangers are real. It is not an accident that there is a general round of wage increases nearly every year, nor that the cost of living has more or less kept pace with the movement of wage rates. With steady high employment, both employers and workers may become less conscious of the need for efficiency. A nation of manufacturers and traders, we may not increase our efficiency fast enough to compete and win in world markets.

How do we keep the great advantage of high employment and avoid these dangers? It is here that the new working principle comes in. To succeed, we have to practise what our governments preach, cultivate restraint, and exert a real self-discipline. It is not something we can do once and for all: as with the other requisites of freedom, we have to keep on at it all the time. After all, the agreed policy of high employment goes a long way to guarantee the interests of both employers and workers. It is no longer enough for them simply to drive hard bargains with each other: they have their common responsibility for the public interest. Where restrictive practices exist on either side of industry, developed in the days when unemployment was widespread and competition really cut-throat, it is time for them to go.

Intelligent Self-Discipline

This issue I am discussing cannot arise in a communist country. If managers are not efficient or workers do not work, they disappear into concentration camps. In a free country with heavy unemployment, the hard discipline of the competitive struggle keeps everyone up to the mark. In our free society, our total democracy, we have chosen freedom both from the compulsion of the state and from the compulsion of want. But the law of the survival of the fittest is always there. We can survive and succeed only if we substitute something positive, the intelligent self-discipline of free men. This is difficult. The democracy we practise is a difficult and demanding way of life. But what is at stake is the future of our society, and at the same time our willingness to grasp our opportunity and be effective in the world.

One of the things which struck my imagination when I lived in the United States was the American attitude to efficient production and technological advance. Americans were fascinated by the scientific technique of continuous discovery. They regarded an idea as old, a technological advance as obsolete, a new product as obsolescent the very moment the idea had been exploited, the improvement carried out, the product made. This is one of the secrets of the American way of life. They feel that perpetual innovation, this ever-repeated assertion of man's power over nature, has an absolute value. They know that in the expanding economy of the United States these activities have paced the development of their country and transformed their standard of living. But there is more to it than that. These activities are a triumphant assertion of the spirit of man.

Most of us do not feel like this. Our traditions are different. We recognise the high place of pure science. For centuries men have found enduring satisfaction in exploring the mysteries of nature. But applied science, engineering, the process of industry – no, these are not on the same footing. Most useful, no doubt, but not inherently distinguished. Indeed we are apt to think that most of the valuable things in life are outside the factory or office. Men really live in their leisure. Work has a subordinate excellence. It should be done well because it is necessary.

Perhaps, but we have to live in the same world with the Americans and compete with them. We have to find an extra bit of purpose and zest over and above the regular motives of daily life. Most people work better if they believe that what they do matters and makes a contribution to their community. If we saw clearly how directly the greatness of Britain depends on our productive efficiency, we should find that extra bit of drive. For making our industries adaptable and flexible is not just the problem of employers and workers. We are all of us involved, for in the end success or failure flows from the climate of opinion, the scale of values of us all.

Take one example. Think of the problem of power, a large

part of productive efficiency. Our workers have at their elbow about one third of the power at the disposal of American workers. We must have more, and it cannot all come from coal. This means developing the industrial uses of nuclear energy and pressing forward fast. And we are well placed. Britain has more than her share of inventive genius: we have a start of ten years over most other countries, except the United States and Russia; and we have an industry big enough to tackle the job. The programme calls for a large and increasing diversion of resources from the immediate comfort and convenience of living. Are we, the voting citizens, ready to choose, and forgo what we would like now, to make sure of the future of Britain?

Or take another illustration, just one of many, the question of working two-day shifts. This is becoming increasingly important in sections of the engineering industry. In order to compete, firms find they must install more complex and costly machinery. But often, if our prices are to be competitive with American prices, the new equipment must be used for more than eight hours a day. You might think this was essentially a specialised matter for industry, for managements and workers. I think not. It is just as much the problem of the whole community. You can see that this must be so. For the different times of starting and stopping work with two shifts a day mean alternations in the whole framework of life. Buses and trains have to run at different times. Shops and restaurants have to alter their hours. Radio and television, the other interests of leisure, have to change their programmes. So it is our problem, too. Are we willing to put ourselves about for the sake of efficiency in industry? We have to choose.

When I began this lecture, I spoke of the opportunity of Britain and the contribution we might make to the settlement of the great problems of the world. I have just been talking of working two shifts a day, shopping hours and bus timetables. I think you may feel this an anticlimax. But is it? It follows the pattern of life. No vision was ever realised except in the humdrum daily round. No hopes ever came true except in the life of every day. The choice for Britain must be made and the job carried out in ordinary life and work. In our free society the vision, the choice and the work are for all. None of us can leave it to others. This is the privilege of freedom, and the enduring responsibility we carry. Britain will continue a Great Power; she will be a leader among the nations and take her part in the great decisions; she will have the economic strength to sustain her role – if we make it our daily business. It is there that we become masters of our fate. Action begins in the workaday world, if we will to be great.

1953

Robert Oppenheimer

~

Science and the Common Understanding

Extract from 'Newton: the Path of Light'

Professor J. Robert Oppenheimer (1904–1967), was an American theoretical physicist whose role in the Manhattan Project during WWII led him to be described as the 'father of the atomic bomb'. His Reith Lecture series examined the impact of quantum and atomic theory on the way societies view themselves and others. In this, his first lecture, he explores how science has advanced over the years, considering the ways in which Isaac Newton's physics and methodologies led to our present rich scientific understanding.

Science has changed the conditions of man's life. It has changed its material conditions; by changing them it has altered our labour and our rest, our power, and the limits of that power, as men and as communities of men, the means and instruments as well as the substance of our learning, the terms and the form in which decisions of right and wrong come before us. It has altered the communities in which we live and cherish, learn and act. It has brought an acute and pervasive sense of change itself into our own life's span. The ideas of science have changed the way men think of themselves and of the world.

The description of these changes is not simple; it is rich in opportunity for error. As for the great material changes which science and practical art have made possible – machines, for instance, or power, the preservation of life, the urbanisation of populations, new instruments of war, new means of communication and information – these are but part of the materials for the analysis of political economy and the wisdom and the insight of history. These are strands in the tangled affairs of men, and their evaluation is no more likely to be final and exhaustive than in any other part of history.

As for the more direct effects of discovery in science on the way men think about things which are not themselves part of science, the historian of ideas has a similar problem. Noting what in actual fact men have said about what they thought, who it was that thought it, and why he thought it, one finds, as in all history, that the contingent and the unpredictable, the peculiar greatnesses and blindnesses of individual men play a determining part. One even finds the science of great scientists taken in the name of those scientists for views and attitudes wholly foreign and sometimes wholly repugnant to them. Both Einstein and Newton created syntheses and insight so compelling and so grand that they induced in professional philosophers a great stir of not always convenient readjustment.

Yet the belief in physical progress, the bright gaiety, and the relative indifference to religion characteristic of the enlightenment, were as foreign to Newton's character and preoccupation as could be; this did not keep the men of the enlightenment from regarding Newton as their patron and prophet. The philosophers and popularisers who have mistaken relativity for the doctrine of relativism have construed Einstein's great works as reducing the objectivity, firmness, and consonance to law of the physical world, whereas it is clear that Einstein has seen in his theories of relativity only a further confirmation of Spinoza's view that it is man's highest function to know and to understand the objective world and its laws.

Often the very fact that the words of science are the same

as those of our common life and tongue can be more mis-leading than enlightening, more frustrating to understanding than recognisably technical jargon. For the words of science– relativity, if you will, or atom, or mutation, or action – have been given a refinement, a precision, and in the end a wholly altered meaning.

Thus we may well be cautious if we enquire as to whether there are direct connections, and if so of what sort, between the truths that science uncovers and the way men think about things in general – their metaphysics – their ideas about what is real and what is primary; their epistemology – their under-standing of what makes human knowledge; their ethics – their ways of thinking, talking, judging and acting in human prob-lems of right and wrong, of good and evil.

These relations, the relations between scientific findings and man's general views, are indeed deep, intimate and subtle. If I did not believe that, I should hardly be addressing these lectures to an attempt to elucidate what there is new in atomic physics that is relevant, helpful and inspiriting for men to know; but the relations are not, I think, relations of logical necessity. This is because science itself is, if not an unmetaphysical, at least a non-metaphysical activity. It takes common sense for granted as well as most of what has gone before in the specialised sciences. And where it adds, alters, or upsets, it does so on the basis of an uncritical acceptance of a great deal else. Thus, to the irritation of many, the assertions of science tend to keep away from the use of words like 'real' and 'ultimate'. The special circumstances of the discovery of scientific truth are never very far from our minds when we expound it, and they act as a protecting sheath against their unlimited and universal acceptance. A few illustrations may make this clearer.

The Underlying Reality

We have discovered atoms. In many ways they act like the atoms of the atomists. They are the stuff of which matter is made; their constellation and motion account for much – in fact, for most of the ordinarily observable properties of matter. But neither they, nor the smaller, less composite particles of which they are made, are permanent, unchanging, or unchangeable. They do not act like objects of fixed form and infinite hardness. Such findings may be persuasive in discouraging the view that the world is made of fixed, immutable, infinitely hard little spheres and other shapes; but such findings are not in the nature of things conclusive, for one may always hold that the true atoms, the immutable, hard atoms, have so far eluded physical discovery but that they are nevertheless there, and only when they are found will physics be dealing with the ultimate reality. Beyond that, one can hold that, although they may never be found by physical experiment, they are the underlying reality in terms of which all else, including the world of physics, is to be understood.

Or, again, we may have discovered that as the nervous impulses pass from the retina of the eye towards the brain itself their geometric disposition resembles less and less that of the object seen. This may complicate or qualify the view that the idea is a geometric replica of the object of vision. It cannot and need not wholly exorcise it.

The scientist may be aware that, whatever his findings, and indeed whatever his field of study, his search for truth is based on communication with other people, on agreement as to results of observation and experiment, and on talking in a common tongue about the instruments and apparatus and objects and procedures which he and others use. He may be aware of the fact that he has learned almost everything he knows from the books and the deeds and talk of other people; and, in so far as these experiences are vivid to him and he is a thoughtful man, he may be hesitant to think that only his own consciousness is real and all else illusion. But that view, too, is not by logic exorcised; from time to time it may rule his spirit.

Although any science gives countless examples of the interrelation of general law and changing phenomena, and although the progress of science has much to do with the enrichment of these relations, knowledge of science and practice of it and interest in it neither compel nor deny the belief that the changing phenomena of the actual world are illusion, that only the unchanging and permanent ideas are real.

If, in the atomic world, we have learned – as we have learned – that events are not causally determined by a strict, efficient, or formal cause; if we have learned to live with this and yet to recognise that for all of the common experience with ordinary bodies and ordinary happenings this atomic lack of causality is of no consequence and no moment, neither the one finding nor the other ensures that men when they think of the world at large are bound to a causal or a non-causal way of thinking.

These many examples show that there can indeed be conflict between the findings of science and what a philosopher or a school of philosophy has said in great particular about some part of experience now accessible to science. But they also show that, if there are relationships between what the sciences reveal about the world and how men think about those parts of it either not yet or never to be explored by science, these are not relationships of logical necessity; they are not relationships which are absolute and compelling, and they are not of such a character that the unity and coherence of an intellectual community can be based wholly upon it.

But if these examples indicate, as we should indeed expect from the nature and conditions of scientific enquiry, that what science finds does not and cannot uniquely determine what men think of as real and as important, they must show as well that there is a kind of relevance – a relevance which will appear different to different men and which will be responsive to many influences outside the work of science. This relevance is a kind of analogy, often of great depth and scope, in which views which have been created or substantiated in some scientific enterprise are similar to those which might be held with regard to metaphysical, epistemological, political, or ethical problems. The success of a critical and sceptical approach in science may encourage a sceptical approach in politics or in ethics; the discovery of an immensely successful theory of great scope may encourage the quest for a simplified view of human institutions. The example of rapid progress in understanding may lead men to conclude that the root of evil is ignorance and that ignorance can be ended.

All these things have happened and all surely will happen again. This means that, if we are to take heart from any beneficent influence that science may have for the common understanding, we need to do so both with modesty and with a full awareness that these relationships are not inevitably and inexorably for man's good.

It is my thesis that generally the new things we have learned in science, and specifically what we have learned in atomic physics, do provide us with valid and relevant and greatly needed analogies to human problems lying outside the present domain of science or its present borderlands. Before I talk of what is new I shall need to sketch, with perhaps an exaggerated simplicity and contrast, the state of knowledge and belief to which these correctives may apply. In doing this, we may have in mind that the general notions about human understanding and community which are illustrated by dis- coveries in atomic physics are not in the nature of things wholly unfamiliar, wholly unheard of or new. Even in our own culture they have a history, and in Buddhist and Hindu thought a more considerable and central place. What we shall find is an exemplification, an encouragement, and a refinement of old wisdom. We shall not need to debate whether, so altered, it is old or new.

There are, then, two sketches that I would like to draw of the background for the altered experience of this century. One is the picture of the physical world that began to take shape in the years between Descartes' birth and Newton's death, that persisted through the eighteenth century, and with immense enrichments and extensions still was the basic picture at the beginning of our own.

The second sketch has to do with the methods, the hopes, the programme, and the style which seventeenth- and eighteenth-century science induced in men of learning and in men of affairs, with some of the special traits of that period of enlightenment which we recognise today as so deep in our tradition, as both so necessary to us and so inadequate.

Physical World as Matter in Motion

More than one great revolution had ended and had been almost forgotten as the seventeenth century drew its picture of the physical world. A centuries-long struggle to decide whether it were rest or uniform motion that was the normal state of an undisturbed body no longer troubled men's minds: the great clarity, so foreign to everyday experience, that motion, as long as it was uniform, needed no cause and no explaining was Newton's first law. The less deep but far more turbulent Copernican revolution was history: the earth revolved about the sun.

The physical world was matter in motion: the motion was to be understood in terms of the impetus or momentum of the bodies which would change only for cause, and of the force that was acting upon it to cause that change. This force was immediate and proximate. It produced a tendency for the impetus to change, and every course could be analysed in terms of the forces deviating bodies from their uniform motions. The physical world was a world of differential law, a world connecting forces and motions at one point and at one instant with those at an infinitely near point in space and point of time; so that the whole course of the physical world could be broken down into finer and finer instants, and in each the cause of change assigned by a knowledge of forces.

Of these forces themselves the greatest in cosmic affairs – that which governed the planets in the heavens and the fall of projectiles on earth – had been found by Newton in the general law of gravity. Was this, too, something that spread from place to place, that was affected only instant by instant, point by point; or was it a property given as a whole, an interaction somehow ordained to exist between bodies remote from one another? Newton was never to answer this question; but he, and even more than he, Huygens, studying the propagation of light, were laying the foundations for a definite view – a view in which the void of the atomists would lose much of its emptiness and take on properties from the bodies which inhabited it, which in turn would affect bodies far away.

It was not until the nineteenth century and Faraday that the full richness of space began to be understood: how it could be the seat not only of gravitational forces produced by the mass of material particles but of electric and magnetic forces produced by their charges. Even in Newton's day it was clear that there were very strong forces at work in lending to material objects their solidity. Newton wrote:

> It seems probable to me, that God in the Beginning form'd Matter in solid, massy, hard, impenetrable, moveable Particles, of such Sizes and Figures, and with such other Properties and in such Proportion to Space, as most conduced to the End for which he formed them; and that these primitive Particles being Solids, are incomparably harder than any porous Bodies compounded of them; even so very hard, as never to wear or break in pieces; no ordinary Power being able to divide what God himself made one in the first Creation.

Newton saw that what held atoms together and made matter must be forces of inordinate strength, and he never considered their existence without a sense of mystery and awe. He did not know, nor do we today know, in what subtle way these forces might or might not be related to the forces of gravity.

But for many of his contemporaries and successors these questions appeared less pressing than the confidence that, once given the forces, the course of nature could be foretold and that, where the laws of gravity could be found, other forces would yield to observation and analysis. It is only in this century that we have begun to come to grips with other instances of antinomy, the apparently irreconcilability between the differential description of nature, point by point, instant to instant, and the total unique law and event. It is only in this century that we have had to recognise how unexpected and unfamiliar that relation between bodies and the atoms on the one hand, and that space full of light and electricity and gravitational forces on the other, could prove to be.

The Eighteenth-century World

For the eighteenth century the world was a giant mechanism. It was a causal world, whether or not gravity and the other forces acting on bodies inhered in them by their nature or by God's will or that they, too, grew, through laws as rigorous as the laws of motion, from the properties induced in space by the bodies in it. All that happened had its full, complete, immediate, efficient cause. The great machine had a determinate course. A knowledge of its present and therefore its future for all time was, in principle, man's to obtain, and perhaps in practice as well. These objects with which the world was filled – the heavenly bodies, the impenetrable atoms and all things composed of them – were found by observation and by experiment; but it would have occurred to no one that their existence and their properties could be qualified or affected by the observations that told of them. The giant machine was not only causal and determinate; it was objective in the sense that no human act or intervention qualified its behaviour.

A physical world so pictured could not but sharpen the great gulf between the object and the idea. It would do much to bring about that long, critical, and, in its later phase, irrational and mystical, view of the relations between the knower and the known that started with Locke and is perhaps even today not fully or happily ended.

It is, of course, clear that many developments in science that were to flower in the eighteenth and nineteenth centuries would soon moderate and complicate the harsh basic picture of the giant machine and of the vast gulf between it and the knowing human mind that thought about it and analysed its properties. This is true of the great development of statistics, which in the end made room for human ignorance as an explicit factor in estimating the behaviour of physical forces. It is true of chemistry, whose phenomena, whatever their ultimate description, looked so very little like the result of matter in motion. It is even more true of the biological sciences, where matter in motion, ever evident and inevitable, appears both at first sight and upon deeper analysis only marginally relevant to what makes biological forms interesting.

But with all of this, and with varying degrees of agreement and reservation, there was the belief that in the end all nature would be reduced to physics, to the giant machine. Despite all the richness of what men have learned about the world of nature, of matter and of space, of change and of life, we carry with us today an image of the giant machine as a sign of what the objective world is really like.

This view of the Newtonian world is over-simplified; perhaps any view of what men made of their new sciences, their new powers, and their new hopes will be simplified to the point of distortion. Science for the eighteenth century was not a finished undertaking; and, if men were overwhelmed with what they had learned, they were easily reminded of how much was still missing. A rational understanding of the world was not an undertaking for one generation or one man, as it is alleged that it at one time appeared to be to Descartes. The immense discoveries of the recent past made it impossible to hold the view that all that was really worth knowing had long been known – a view that is a sort of parody, in my case, of the Renaissance.

Man's Long Journey of Discovery

This was a long journey on which men were embarked, the journey of discovery; they would need their wits and their resources and their forbearance if they were to get on with it. But it was a job in which progress was inevitable, and in which the style and success of physical science would tend to set the style for all undertakings of man's reason. What there is of direct borrowing from Newtonian physics for chemistry, psychology, or politics is mostly crude and sterile. What there is in eighteenth-century political and economic theory that derives from Newtonian methodology is hard for even an earnest reader to find. The absence of experiment and the inapplicability of Newtonian methods of mathematical analysis make that inevitable. These were not what physical science meant to the enlightenment.

It meant a style of thought, a habit of success, and an understanding of community quite typical for the age. These are to be found best in the learned communities that grew up in Europe and later in America – in the Royal Society and in the far more ambitious, far more revolutionary, far more programmatic French Academy. These communities were infused by a confidence in the power of reason and by a sense of improvement constant and almost inevitable in the condition of man's knowledge, and therefore of his actions and his life. They rest on a consensus of men, often seeing with their own eyes the crucial experiment that was to test or to confirm a theory; on the common experience of criticism and analysis; on the widespread use of mathematical methods with all the assurance of objectivity and precision that they give us. These were communities banded together for the promotion of knowledge – critical, rapacious to correct error, yet tolerant from knowing that error is an inevitable step in acquiring new knowledge. These were communities proud of their broad, non-sectarian, international membership, proud of their style and their wit, and with a wonderful sense of new freedom. One may recapture some sense of these communities from the writings of the time. The first history of the Royal Society is not truly a history but an apology, written when the society was only a few years old, explaining it, defending it against its critics. Bishop Sprat has this to say:

> Their purpose is, in short, to make faithful *Records* of all the Works of *Nature*, or *Art*, which can come within their Reach; that so the present Age, and posterity, may be able to put a mark on the Errors, which have been strengthened by long prescription; to restore the Truths, that have lain neglected; to push on those, which are already known, to more various uses; and to make the way more passable, to what remains unreveal'd. This is the compass of their Design . . .
>
> They have try'd to put it into a condition of perpetual increasing, by settling an inviolable correspondence

between the hand and the brain. They have studied, to make it not only an Enterprise of one season, or of some lucky opportunity; but a business of time; a steady, a lasting, a popular, an uninterrupted Work . . .

It is to be noted, that they have freely admitted Men of different Religions, Countries, and Professions of Life. This they were oblig'd to do, or else they would come far short of the largeness of their own Declarations. For they openly profess, not to lay the Foundation of an *English*, *Scotch*, *Irish*, *Popish*, or *Protestant* Philosophy; but a Philosophy of *Mankind*.

Reading this today, we can hardly escape a haunting sense of its timeliness and a certain nostalgia at how little the texture of our life conforms to these agreeable and noble ideals. We cannot perhaps wholly forget how much these communities owed to the long centuries of Christian life and Christian tradition; how much that they then took for granted in their enquiries and thoughts, in their whole style, derived from a way of life and a history which they were about to change beyond all recognition; and how deeply this, their programme, could alter the very men and the very minds to whom their programme would in time become entrusted.

These, however, were not reflections to darken much the eighteenth-century or to cast real shadows on that great path of light, that renewed hope of men for a growing and growingly rational comprehension of their world and of themselves. At the very end of the century in another land largely nourished and fathered by the enlightenment, a gentleman and patriot wrote a letter. He wrote in answer to a young friend enquiring about his present course of study. He wrote in the last days of the Directorate, when the course of history was diverging in alarming and immense ways from that charted by the men of the French Academy. He wrote it about two years before he was to assume the Presidency of the United States, there for over a century to raise more firmly than ever before the standard of man's freedom, his progress, and his rational nature.

> I am among those who think well of the human character generally. I consider man as formed for society, and endowed by nature with those dispositions which fit him for society. I believe also, with Condorcet, as mentioned in your letter, that his mind is perfectible to a degree of which we cannot as yet form any conception science can never be retrograde; what is once acquired of real knowledge can never be lost. To preserve the freedom of the human mind then and freedom of the press, every spirit should be ready to devote himself to martyrdom; for as long as we may think as we will, and speak as we think, the condition of man will proceed in improvement.
>
> The generation which is going off the stage has deserved well of mankind for the struggles it has made, and for having arrested that course of despotism which

had overwhelmed the world for thousands and thousands of years. If there seems to be danger that the ground they have gained will be lost again, that danger comes from the generation your contemporary. But that the enthusiasm which characterises youth should lift its parricide hands against freedom and science would be such a monstrous phenomenon as I cannot place among possible things in this age and country.

The writer of the letter was Thomas Jefferson.

The Reith Lectures in full, 1948–2019

2004   Wole Soyinka, *Climate of Fear*

2005   Alec Broers, *The Triumph of Technology*

2006   Daniel Barenboim, *In the Beginning was Sound*

2007   Jeffrey Sachs, *Bursting at the Seams*

2008   Jonathan Spence, *Chinese Vistas*

2009   Michael Sandel, *A New Citizenship*

2010   Martin Rees, *Scientific Horizons*

2011   Aung San Suu Kyi and Baroness Manningham-Buller, *Securing Freedom*

2012   Niall Ferguson, *The Rule of Law and Its Enemies*

2013   Grayson Perry, *Playing to the Gallery*

2014   Dr Atul Gawande, *The Future of Medicine*

2016   Professor Stephen Hawking, *Black Holes*; plus Kwame Anthony Appiah, *Mistaken Identities*

2017   Hilary Mantel, *Resurrection: The Art and Craft*

2018   Margaret MacMillan, *The Mark of Cain*

2019   Jonathan Sumption, *Law and the Decline of Politics*

ACKNOWLEDGEMENTS AND CREDITS

The publisher would like to thank the BBC, especially Ellie Caddell, Eleanor Bishop, Ewan Billinge, Gill Carter, Hugh Levinson, Gwyneth Williams and Anita Anand. The lectures have been reproduced by kind permission of the copyright holders and licensed by the BBC.

Foreword (p. vii), © Anita Anand
Introduction (p. xvii), © Gwyneth Williams
Law and the Decline of Politics (p. 1), © Jonathan Sumption
Resurrection: the Art and Craft (p. 17), © Hilary Mantel
Securing Freedom (p. 31), © Eliza Manningham-Buller (Profile Books, 2012)
Scientific Horizons (p. 45), © Martin Rees
Bursting at the Seams (p. 61), © Jeffrey Sachs
In the Beginning was Sound (p. 75), © Daniel Barenboim
The Triumph of Technology (p. 85), © Alec Broers
The Emerging Mind (p. 99), © V. S. Ramachandran (Profile Books, 2003)
Respect for the Earth (p. 111), © HRH The Prince of Wales
Sustainable City (p. 123), © Richard Rogers
The Persistence of Faith (p. 141), © Jonathan Sacks
Law, Justice and Democracy (p. 157), © John McCluskey
Change in British Society (p. 175), © A.H. Halsey
Mechanics of the Mind (p. 193), © Colin Blakemore
Europe: Journey to an Unknown Destination (p. 213), © Andrew Shonfield
Only Connect (p. 229), © Richard Hoggart
The Age of Automation (p. 247), © Leon Bagrit
Britain and the Tide of World Affairs (p. 265), © Oliver Franks
Science and the Common Understanding (p. 281), © Robert Oppenheimer

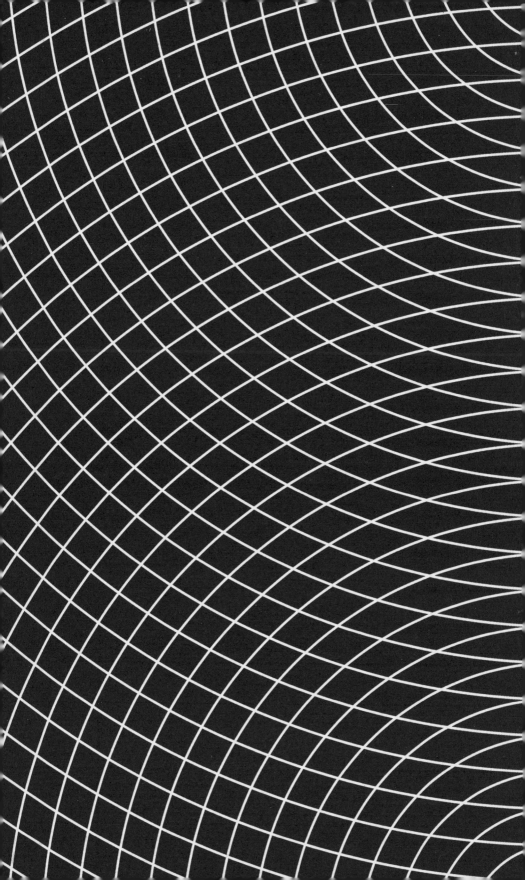